Albert Einstein

Mileva Marić

 *The Love Letters*

EDITED AND WITH AN
INTRODUCTION BY
JÜRGEN RENN AND
ROBERT SCHULMANN

TRANSLATED BY
SHAWN SMITH

PRINCETON UNIVERSITY PRESS

PRINCETON AND OXFORD

Copyright © 1992 by Princeton University Press
Published by Princeton University Press, 41 William Street,
Princeton, New Jersey 08540
In the United Kingdom: Princeton University Press,
3 Market Place, Woodstock, Oxfordshire OX20 1SY

Second printing, and first paperback printing, 2001
Paperback ISBN 0-691-08886-1

*The Library of Congress has cataloged the cloth edition
of this book as follows*

Einstein, Albert, 1879–1955.
[Correspondence. English. Selections]
Albert Einstein/Mileva Marić—the love letters / with
an introduction by Jürgen Renn and Robert Schulmann ;
translated from the German by Shawn Smith.
p.   cm.
Includes bibliographical references.
ISBN 0-691-08760-1
1. Einstein, Albert, 1879–1955—Correspondence.
2. Einstein-Marić, Mileva, 1875–1948—Correspondence.
3. Physicists—Correspondence. I. Einstein—Marić, Mileva,
1875–1948. II. Renn, Jürgen, 1956– . III. Schulmann,
Robert J., 1942– . IV. Smith, Shawn, 1968– . V. Title.
VI. Title: Love letters.
QC16.E5A4   1992
530″.092—dc20   91-40183

This book has been composed in Adobe Times Roman
Designed by Jan Lilly

Printed on acid-free paper. ∞

www.pup.princeton.edu

Printed in the United States of America

10 9 8 7 6 5 4 3 2

The imagination of a boy is healthy, and the mature imagination of a man is healthy; but there is a space of life between, in which the soul is in a ferment, the character undecided, the way of life uncertain, the ambition thick-sighted: thence proceeds mawkishness, and all the thousand bitters which those men I speak of must necessarily taste in going over the following pages.

John Keats, Preface to *Endymion* (1818)

Contents

&

Foreword, by Martin J. Klein		*ix*
Introduction		*xi*
Textual Note		*xxix*
Translator's Note		*xxxi*

The Letters:

1	Marić to Einstein, after 20 October 1897	*3*
2	Einstein to Marić, 16 February 1898	*4*
3	Einstein to Marić, after 16 April 1898	*6*
4	Einstein to Marić, after 16 April 1898	*6*
5	Einstein to Marić, after 28 November 1898	*7*
6	Einstein to Marić, 13 or 20 March 1899	*7*
7	Einstein to Marić, early August 1899	*9*
8	Einstein to Marić, 10? August 1899	*10*
9	Marić to Einstein, after 10 August–before 10 September 1899	*12*
10	Einstein to Marić, 10 September 1899	*13*
11	Einstein to Marić, 28? September 1899	*15*
12	Einstein to Marić, 10 October 1899	*17*
13	Marić to Einstein, 1900?	*18*
14	Einstein to Marić, 29? July 1900	*19*
15	Einstein to Marić, 1 August 1900	*21*
16	Einstein to Marić, 6 August 1900	*22*
17	Einstein to Marić, 9? August 1900	*24*
18	Einstein to Marić, 14? August 1900	*25*
19	Einstein to Marić, 20 August 1900	*27*
20	Einstein to Marić, 30 August or 6 September 1900	*29*
21	Einstein to Marić, 13? September 1900	*31*
22	Einstein to Marić, 19 September 1900	*33*
23	Einstein to Marić, 3 October 1900	*35*

24 Einstein to Marić, 23 March 1901   36
25 Einstein to Marić, 27 March 1901   38
26 Einstein to Marić, 4 April 1901   41
27 Einstein to Marić, 10 April 1901   42
28 Einstein to Marić, 15 April 1901   44
29 Einstein to Marić, 30 April 1901   46
30 Marić to Einstein, 2 May 1901   48
31 Marić to Einstein, 3 May 1901   49
32 Einstein to Marić, 9 May 1901   50
33 Einstein to Marić, second half of May? 1901   51
34 Marić to Einstein, second half of May? 1901   52
35 Einstein to Marić, second half of May? 1901   53
36 Einstein to Marić, 28? May 1901   54
37 Einstein to Marić, 4? June 1901   55
38 Einstein to Marić, 7? July 1901   56
39 Marić to Einstein, ca. 8 July 1901   57
40 Einstein to Marić, 22? July 1901   59
41 Marić to Einstein, 31? July 1901   60
42 Marić to Einstein, early November 1901   62
43 Marić to Einstein, 13 November 1901   63
44 Einstein to Marić, 28 November 1901   65
45 Einstein to Marić, 12 December 1901   66
46 Einstein to Marić, 17 December 1901   69
47 Einstein to Marić, 19 December 1901   70
48 Einstein to Marić, 28 December 1901   72
49 Einstein to Marić, 4 February 1902   73
50 Einstein to Marić, 8? February 1902   75
51 Einstein to Marić, 17? February 1902   76
52 Einstein to Marić, 28 June 1902 or later   77
53 Einstein-Marić to Einstein, 27 August 1903   78
54 Einstein to Einstein-Marić, 19? September 1903   78

Notes   81

Literature Cited   103

Foreword

ॐ

This collection of letters introduces us to an Einstein we had not previously known. The familiar Einstein, whose image produces instant recognition throughout the world, is the patriarchal figure who spent the last two decades of his life in Princeton, working on his never-completed unified field theory and giving his support to a variety of valiant efforts to preserve rationality in a world that sadly needs it. The scientist's Einstein, from whom this patriarch developed, is the younger man who between 1905 and 1925 created much of the conceptual and theoretical structure on which the physics of our century has been built. But what we have here is a youth just in the process of becoming Albert Einstein, and for that reason an extremely interesting youth.

As this series of letters begins in 1897, the eighteen-year-old Einstein is in his second year as a student at the Swiss Federal Polytechnic, enthusiastic about what he is learning and eager to share his ideas and reactions with his fellow student, Mileva Marić, in whom he is becoming seriously interested. As their relationship develops and deepens, he writes to her freely and openly about much that is going on inside him—his feelings about her, his family, and himself, and his thoughts about the life he sees around him and the life he wants to live with her. Because Marić shared at least some of his scientific interests and his love for his subject, Einstein also tells her about his reading and about the scientific ideas stimulated, provoked, and set free by this reading. We also get to know Marić through her own letters, and we see the maturity, independence, and strength that Einstein valued so highly at this time.

During the six years spanned by these letters, Einstein and Marić lived through much together. By 1903 they are married, she is pregnant, and Einstein is established in his position at the Swiss Patent Office, promising to "get ahead" so that they "don't have to starve."[1] His scientific career has already begun and will shortly burst forth in the great works of 1905; her plans for a career have apparently been abandoned. Their marriage would not survive for much more than a decade, despite the promise manifest in these letters.

Even a casual reading of this correspondence will show what a rich source it provides for extending our understanding of Einstein's development. The probing and suggestive Introduction by Jürgen Renn and Robert Schulmann sets these letters in a number of contexts and shows how they can be mined by scholars.

Richard Ellmann once wrote: "The controlled seething out of which great works come is not likely to yield all its secrets."[2] He was referring to literary works, but his remark applies just as well to scientific ones. Nevertheless, a correspondence like the one presented here goes a long way toward helping us see where that "controlled seething" has its start.

Martin J. Klein

[1] Letter 54.

[2] Ellmann, Richard. *Golden Codgers: Biographical Speculations* (New York and London: Oxford University Press, 1973), p. 16.

Introduction

🐦

Publishing love letters necessarily raises a variety of expectations among readers and some hesitation on the part of editors and publishers to infringe on a private sphere. While the letters may allow a reader to intrude into past intimacies and passions, they may on the other hand serve only as indecipherable remnants of sentiments and experiences that were shared and then faded long ago, or reveal lives trapped in a humdrum routine masked by emotional phrasing. If one is lucky, however, as we are in the case of the correspondence between the young Albert Einstein and Mileva Marić, love letters introduce their reader to wellsprings of emotional and intellectual development of the correspondents, wellsprings that are inaccessible through other sources.

The letters in this volume compel a change in our understanding of the early relationship between Albert and Mileva and of their common apprenticeship in physics. Although insights into their relationship are limited by the relatively few occasions when separation of the two lovers led to an exchange of letters, numerous themes are touched upon that provide glimpses into their mutual concerns. One of the surprises is the extent to which Mileva—usually depicted as an incidental shadow of Albert's early years—can be observed sharing his scientific enthusiasm and interests. But while, at first sight, the fifty-four love letters presented here promise to unlock the secrets of Mileva's personality and of her role in the developing field of theoretical physics, we are, on closer inspection, disappointed by the small number of letters from her—only eleven out of the fifty-four. In all probability, Albert carelessly discarded some of the letters he received from Mileva. We are also struck from the outset by an asymmetry in the voices of the two lovers—his, self-assured, dramatic, masterful in the command of his native German; hers, often understated, self-effacing, tentative in a language foreign to her native Serbian—which inevitably mars our perception of the relationship. Fragmentary and personal as the love letters are, they make it difficult to decipher Mileva's enigmatic personality. Extensive research is needed into her background and into the cultural and social context in which this extraordinary young woman, the only female student of physics in her university class, searched for a role in life.

Just as a slim volume of love letters cannot offer a coherent view of Mileva Marić's life, it cannot provide answers to all questions biographers, historians of science, and the interested layman may pose concerning the intellectual contributions of both Mileva and Albert. What we propose to do in this introduction, instead of separating out the different strands of their science and their romance, is to touch on some of the themes relevant to both. This correspondence, we believe, affords a new understanding of the combination of intellectual and emotional resources that made possible Einstein's path-breaking contributions of his miraculous year, the *annus mirabilis* of 1905.

The publication of Einstein's three fundamental contributions to three different areas of physics in 1905 is a unique event in the history of science. In this one year, a young man of twenty-six years of age changed forever our accepted view of the physical world. He introduced the revolutionary concept of light quanta, an idea that conflicts with one of the most well-established physical theories of the nineteenth century—the wave theory of light—and opened the way to the development of modern quantum theory. Only weeks after making this contribution, Einstein, who at the time was only a junior civil servant in the Swiss Patent Office, submitted his explanation of Brownian motion for publication. The phenomenon itself had probably been known since the time when microscopes were invented in the seventeenth century, but several generations of botanists, physiologists, and physicists had struggled in vain to find the cause of this irregular and unceasing motion of very small bodies suspended in a liquid. In one stroke, Einstein's explanation cleared the path for the acceptance of molecular reality. Finally, only a month later, Einstein submitted what is no doubt the greatest of his early contributions, the special theory of relativity. The intellectual culture of our time cannot be fully understood without taking into account the impact of this theory. Not only the electrodynamics of moving bodies, but every physical theory that has been formulated since then has had to confront Einstein's revolutionary changes in the notions of space and time.

What do we know about the circumstances of this revolution, and what of the young man who launched it? Historians of science and Einstein himself in his later reminiscences refer us to the giants on whose shoulders he stood, and there can be no doubt that the masters of late nineteenth-century physics—Planck, Lorentz, Boltzmann, and others—created the preconditions for Einstein's path-breaking contributions. But these achievements, although based on prior results, should still be recognized as the triumph of new concepts rather than as a merely technical refinement of earlier accomplishments.

How could a young man who had only recently received a secondary-school teaching certificate see that which remained obscure to masters in the field? Our historical access to the revolutionary Einstein has until recently been rather limited. For the most part it relied on his later recollections, on the accounts of those who met and knew him, on administrative records, and on a modest collection of his correspondence from this period. There are virtually no contemporary sources on the prehistory of the 1905 publications. Drafts of these papers have not survived, nor are extensive discussions of their contents available from Einstein's early correspondence.

The situation has markedly improved since a systematic examination and presentation of his papers and correspondence was organized in the early 1980s under the direction of John Stachel. This editorial project was conceived in part as an archaeological enterprise whose success depended on the interplay of historical interpretation and archival fieldwork. It was by dint of such a combined effort that the letters presented in this volume were uncovered in 1986 with the gracious assistance of Einstein's granddaughter Evelyn Einstein, who first drew our attention to their existence. These letters, all dating from the crucial years before Einstein made his revolutionary contributions to physics, have dramatically enhanced our chances of giving plausible answers to the question posed above. But where did these letters come from?

On Mileva's death in 1948, her literary effects were transferred from Switzerland to the United States, where her oldest son Hans Albert was a professor of hydraulic engineering at the University of California at Berkeley. After divorcing Albert in 1919, Mileva had maintained her residence in Zurich until the end of her life and never remarried. Though the divorce proceedings were very bitter, a reconciliation of sorts was achieved by the late twenties, and in the last two decades of her life several hundreds of letters were exchanged between Mileva and Albert, which will appear interspersed in future volumes of the *Collected Papers of Albert Einstein*.

The letters presented here comprise the surviving correspondence of their courtship and were written at the turn of the century. The first was written a year after the couple began their studies together (1897) and the last two are from the year of their marriage (1903). The various locations in which the letters were written reflect the footloose life of the correspondents. The first is from Heidelberg in 1897, where Mileva spent the winter semester 1897–1898. Others are from Zurich, where both lived while attending the Swiss Federal Polytechnic (ETH); from Milan, where Albert's parents lived; from Mileva's home in what was then southern Hungary, now the Voivodina region of Yugoslavia; from Winterthur and Schaffhausen in Switzerland, where Albert held temporary teaching jobs; from Stein am Rhein on the Swiss-German border, where Mileva briefly stayed at a dramatic point in her life; from resorts in Switzerland, where Albert vacationed with his mother and sister; and from Bern, where he finally found a secure position at the Swiss Patent Office in 1902.

Almost twenty-one years old, Mileva entered the ETH in 1896, the same year as Einstein, who was three-and-a-half years her junior. She was, in that year, the only woman beginning studies in the mathematical section of the School for Mathematics and Science Teachers. In her first letter, written from Heidelberg, she shows her fascination with a lecture in which the German experimental physicist Philipp Lenard has explained the relationship between the mean velocity of a molecule and the average distance traversed by it between collisions, a topic that was later to become relevant in Einstein's studies of Brownian motion. Her early letters to Einstein indicate a high degree of self-consciousness and independence, discipline in her studies, and a healthy measure of impudence. On one occasion she deigns to grant him a letter, mimics his use of south German dialect, and pokes fun at the pomposity of German professors. But while the saucy tone in her earlier letters is not unlike that displayed in so many letters by Einstein himself in this period and throughout his life, her sense of isolation as the only female student in her class is almost palpable, and her later letters are often characterized by a fatalistic tone, and unfortunately give little indication of how her scientific interests were developing.

The correspondence reveals for the first time some of the dramatic moments in Mileva's life—events that forced her into the background of Einstein's success story. In 1901 Mileva attempted for the second time to obtain her teaching certificate from the ETH and was again unsuccessful. Six months later she gave birth to a daughter fathered by Albert. At the time neither of the baby Lieserl's parents had a secure income. The birth of the illegitimate girl made their situation even more precarious, since it endangered Einstein's chances of gaining a position in the stuffy social environment of Switzerland's capital, Bern. Be that as it may, Lieserl was born and spent her childhood far from Switzerland, probably in the care of Mileva's relatives in the area which Mileva called home. The letters between Lieserl's parents allow one to speculate that she was eventually given up for adoption and that a friend of Mileva's may have been helpful in arranging the matter. Lieserl was never to be mentioned again in any of the surviving letters, and all attempts to find clues about her later life have failed. What we do know is that on June 16, 1902, Albert began a provisional appointment as a Technical Expert, third class, at the Swiss Patent Office in Bern, and that half a year later he married Mileva there.

Little was known about the youthful Mileva before the letters presented here were uncovered. Beyond the facts that she was of Serbian ethnic origin, was the daughter of a prosperous Hungarian civil servant, before coming to Switzerland had received special dispensation to attend courses in mathematics and physics at an all-male secondary school in Zagreb, and had begun her Swiss university training in medicine—information for which we are indebted to the earlier research of two Serbian biographers—not much more can be gleaned.

The life of the young Albert, on the other hand, or "the corpse of my childhood," as he once mockingly referred to it, has been relatively well explored. His family had offered him a background rich in occasions for the intellectual development that prepared him for his later study of physics. Born in Ulm in southern Germany in 1879, he grew up in Munich, where his father and uncle owned an electrotechnical enterprise in which dynamos, electric meters, arc and incandescent lamps, telephone systems, and the like were produced. By the start of Albert's correspondence with Mileva, his father had moved the business to northern Italy, a region that was experiencing rapid economical and industrial development at the turn of the century. Not many firms in the capital-intensive electrotechnical business could survive the tough competition with larger enterprises, and the firms founded by Hermann Einstein, first in Munich, then in Pavia, then in Milan, were all liquidated after a few years. The financial problems of the family weighed heavily on Albert, the only son. They are a significant factor in his decision to pursue a career in engineering when he made his first attempt at entering the ETH in 1895 at the age of sixteen.

Some of Einstein's earliest experiences with science in childhood and adolescence, experiences he remembered half a century later when he wrote an autobiographical sketch, had their origin in the electrotechnical setting of the family business. As a precocious adolescent, he wrote a scientific essay on the state of the ether in a magnetic field and sent it to a favorite uncle. His long-standing interests in problems of the ether and in electrodynamics are also evident in his letters to Mileva, where he calls them his "hobby horses"

(Letter 10) and is at first afraid to bore her with these topics, but then draws her more and more into his fascination with them.

By the time Einstein began his studies at the ETH, he had left behind the period in which his family could provide him with intellectual stimulation. But the emotional ties, with his mother Pauline and his sister Maja in particular, as well as a sense of obligation to his father, remained as strong as they were ambivalent. His parents opposed the liaison with Mileva and attempted more than once to end it. Yet Albert visited his parents frequently or spent vacations with them even in times of high tension and open conflict over his relationship with Mileva or, as he referred to it, the "Dollie affair." In Letter 14 he attempts to demonstrate—to Mileva and possibly to himself—his casual superiority in dealing with maternal opposition by describing a scene in his mother's bedroom at a resort hotel, where he tells his mother of his intention to marry Mileva. His sarcastic and colorful depiction of a middle-class matron, desperate at the thought of losing her only son to a woman of lower station, certainly reflects some of Pauline Einstein's objections to this *mésalliance*. More telling is the reflection on its author. Einstein's sense of theater and dramatic flair are evident and he fully exploits a situation that allows him to declare his steadfastness and love while ridiculing the philistine protests of his mother. Mileva's reaction to parental opposition is more matter-of-fact, and she repeatedly counsels Albert to hold his fire. Grudgingly, he comes to acknowledge his lover's emotional maturity in the matter and admits that it would have been better had he held his tongue. This volubility seems never to have left Einstein, although in later years it was cloaked in the self-imposed reticence of the wise man. In 1912, in preparing a friend for a first encounter with Einstein, the physicist Max von Laue said: "You should be careful that Einstein doesn't talk you to death. He loves to do that, you know."

In embarking on his romance with Mileva, Albert decided in favor of a relationship with an emotionally and intellectually mature woman. Even as he began courting Mileva, he was turning his back on an earlier affair. After failing to gain entrance to the ETH in 1895, Albert spent a year in the town of Aarau, a short distance from

Zurich. There he attended the final year of secondary school, and it was there that he also had his first romance, one of which his mother seems to have approved. It was with Marie Winteler, daughter of the schoolteacher Jost Winteler, in whose home Albert boarded while attending school across the street. Two years older than Albert, Marie did not seek an intellectual partnership with her friend. Instead she refers to herself in a letter to him as "the little, insignificant, foolish darling that can neither do, nor understand anything." After Albert had moved on to Zurich and met Mileva, he still sent Marie his dirty laundry and she mailed it back to him. Together with his new Serbian girlfriend, whose calm independence and intellectual ambition he admired, he sought to create a bond of intellectual companionship that was impervious to the petty concerns and hopes of innocent puppy love. He considered himself lucky to have found Mileva, "a creature who is my equal, and who is as strong and independent as I am!" (Letter 23). But at the same time, he also saw in her a lover with whom he could withdraw into their little student "household" in Zurich, or enjoy a trip into the Swiss Alps, free from worries and ambitions.

While the letters of this volume cast a new light on Mileva and on Albert's early relationship with her, this seems at first glance to be far less the case for Einstein, the promising scientist, whose image is so well defined by later reminiscences. But for the first time we are able to reconstruct the youthful Einstein with an unprecedented immediacy from these contemporary letters documenting his intellectual development in the midst of the conflicts of his adolescence. For instance, we find that the rebelliousness and theatrical attitude in his personal life are paralleled in his developing self-image as a lonely revolutionary of science. This is most clearly evident in his description of his first scientific polemics, on which he proudly reports to Mileva. In 1901, Albert had at first reacted with enthusiam to Professor Paul Drude's publication of an electron theory of metals, in which the phenomena of heat and electrical conduction are both explained by an "electron gas," conceived in analogy to the kinetic theory of gases. He had earlier thought of this analogy himself, and the twenty-two-year-old Einstein thus considered Drude a colleague, an equal with whom he could argue privately over particulars. On writing a letter to Drude containing two "factual objections," he received a dismissive response indicating that Drude thought otherwise. To an intellectual father figure, Einstein now confides that he will "soon make things hot for the man" by publishing his objections, and then he categorically proclaims that unthinking respect for authority is the greatest enemy of truth.

Although Einstein never published the promised attacks on Drude, he had already brought acts of defiance and independence to successful conclusions. At age fifteen he decided without consulting his parents to leave his high school in Munich, probably to avoid military service. This gesture of independence greatly frightened the older Einsteins, but his equally independent decision to apply to the engineering division at the ETH appears to have mollified them. Yet when he failed the entrance examination, it seemed that he had bitten off more than he could chew. Luckily, a family connection in the small town of Aarau helped him to spend a year at an exceptionally modern and well-equipped institution of learning, the Aargau cantonal high school. Its liberal spirit and the simple dedication of the teachers, who refused to rely on external authority, deeply impressed Einstein. It is generally agreed that the time in Aarau was of considerable importance for him. Although we know that some of his teachers were not only schoolteachers but researchers in their own right—in linguistics, in geology, and in physics—it has remained unclear what exactly their contribution to his intellectual development was, mainly because there was hardly any contemporary evidence of relevance to this development between Einstein's time in Aarau and the *annus mirabilis* of 1905.

Does the correspondence with Mileva offer new clues about the role of the various intellectual influences on Einstein? Does it offer a missing link in the development leading to 1905? If we examine the correspondence for the roots of the revolutionary papers of that year, and for those of relativity in particular, we must conclude that the letters do not enable us to reconstruct in detail the development from some of Einstein's well-known youthful speculations to his later contributions. But the letters do show how the interest in electrodynamics—Einstein's avocation since the age of sixteen—has now become more specific, and that it is already focused on the topics that would mark his later fundamental contribution: the electrodynamics of moving bodies, the problematic character of the notion of the ether, and the relativity principle. The earliest letters in this volume already show him studying the contemporary literature. Here he expresses his doubts about the concept of ether motion and has an idea about the effect of relative motion with respect to the ether on light propagation, while at the same time conceiving an experiment to investigate light propagation in transparent bodies moving with respect to the ether. Unfortunately, the letters do not specify precisely why Einstein had doubts regarding the motion of the ether, what the idea about motion relative to the ether was, and what particular experiment he was contemplating.

For almost two years the topic of electrodynamics of moving bodies surfaces only in passing references in Albert's letters—and does not appear in Mileva's at all—but his unceasing interest in the subject as well as the fact that he continues to discuss it with Mileva and with his friends Michele Besso and Marcel Grossmann can be taken for granted. In the spring of 1901, he discussed key problems such as the separation of ether and matter and the definition of absolute rest with Besso; a month earlier, he had even written to Mileva about "our work on relative motion" (Letter 25). At the end of the year he was working on what he expected to become a major treatise on the electrodynamics of moving bodies, a paper that apparently included a proposal for investigating the motion of matter relative to the ether. We do not know the content of the planned treatise, just as we do not know Mileva's possible contribution to it; but whatever it was, all available evidence indicates that the planned paper was a far cry from the relativity paper of 1905.

The passing references to the relativity theme do not constitute a Rosetta stone for deciphering its history. On the other hand, the letters are full of references to ideas, research projects, library work, and planned experiments that have no direct bearing on the path-breaking achievements of the *annus mirabilis.* This wealth of description would make the love letters between Albert and Mileva intellectually exciting even if none of the 1905 papers had ever been written. Many of the references to science are related in one way or another to what Einstein later called his worthless beginner papers. Molecular forces, thermoelectricity, physical chemistry, and the kinetic theory of gases and liquids are, together with electrodynamics, the most prominent scientific subjects in the correspondence with Mileva. In spite of his later negative assessment, he is clearly fascinated by all of these topics, some of which he first encounters in his course work at the ETH. The important role that Einstein's ETH physics professor, H. F. Weber, played in the development of his student's scientific interests is just one among many new insights these letters afford us. Einstein's reminiscences of later years speak almost exclusively of the clash between the rebellious and independent-minded student of theoretical physics and the established experimental physicist and argue that it was unavoidable from the beginning. The possibility that the brilliant young man could have been intellectually stimulated by Weber with his somewhat outmoded physics curriculum is rarely considered.

The letters also throw a new light on the clash that was brewing between Einstein and Weber. Whereas students under Weber's supervision usually focused their research on work in the laboratory, we see Einstein relying on tables and experimental results published by others rather than engaging in experimental projects himself. The boldness with which Einstein attempts to establish connections between seemingly unrelated data also characterizes some of his later and more successful contributions to physics. While at the ETH, his theoretical ambitions had indeed come to outweigh his initial involvement with experimental research. But Weber, for his part, perhaps became increasingly dissatisfied with the unorthodox student who cut too many corners. As a consequence of the antagonism, Einstein gave up a first attempt at a dissertation, while Weber, at least from Einstein's point of view, stopped at nothing to sabotage the young man's search for a job after graduation.

Still, the constraints imposed by the empirical orientation at Weber's ETH physics institute may have been a healthy influence on an ambitious, budding theoretician. In all of Einstein's fundamental contributions of 1905, a strong awareness of the experimentally controllable implications can be observed. It seems only fair to ask whether it is Einstein's technical orientation, stimulated first by the family background in electrotechnology and then by his attendance at a technical university, that helps to distinguish his innovative contributions to theoretical physics from the work of contemporary mathematical physicists such as Boltzmann. As a matter of fact, in one letter to Mileva, Albert tells her that he really admires Boltzmann's gas theory but finds that "not enough emphasis is placed on a comparison with reality" (Letter 29).

It would, of course, be too simplistic to assume that one or the other "influence" on Einstein could explain his intellectual development. The well-known image of Einstein the autodidact is confirmed by the correspondence, and we can observe firsthand the array of texts he consulted. We see him reading, together with Mileva, the classic works of Boltzmann, Drude, Helmholtz, Hertz, Kirchhoff, Mach, and Ostwald, in addition to the notebooks of his fellow student, Grossmann, and we can reconstruct from Einstein's later contributions the important role this reading had on his education. But we also see how he selects with an impressive sovereignty those aspects of the readings he felt to be essential. Thus he was convinced that the principles of Boltzmann's theory were correct, yet he would not become a blind follower of its mathematical program. He would read Ostwald, the anti-atomist, with as much profit as he read Boltzmann, the atomist. He would carefully study Mach's arguments against burdening physics with unnecessary concepts and eventually discard the ether concept, while accepting Mach's criticism of atomism as a challenge and trying to provide evidence for the existence of atoms.

What is it that enabled Einstein to assimilate the writings of these seemingly disparate intellectual masters with such judiciousness? When one attempts to reconstruct how he developed, as he later wrote, an eye for the intrinsically significant in the course of his studies, one should remember that the various intellectual stimuli mentioned in the correspondence fell onto fertile ground. One of the hidden sources for his preparation in physics, mentioned only in passing in the letters but given prominence fifty years later in autobiographical notes, is the popular compendium on the natural sciences by Aaron Bernstein, written in the middle of the nineteenth century.

The topics treated by Bernstein contain striking parallels to some of Einstein's ideas. Bernstein discusses the corpuscular theory of light that Einstein would revive with his light quantum hypothesis, and he even mentions the possibility of light deflection by a gravitational field, eventually one of the key proofs of the general theory of relativity. Closer to Einstein's early interests, Bernstein unfolds the theme of atoms and the "secret" forces acting between them into an all-encompassing panorama of the unity of nature. Although such a picture could no longer do justice to the complexities of science at the turn of the century, it provided the background for one of Einstein's earliest research programs—that of exploring the analogy between molecular forces and gravitation.

Einstein's creativity can be explained as little by his reading on his own of popular science texts as it can by the stimulation he later derived from Weber's courses. But the fact that Einstein had a broad conceptual understanding of physics before he started to assimilate the more technical knowledge—for instance, in Weber's courses—gave him an intellectual independence with respect to what he learned, the possibility of picking and choosing from the manifold of knowledge with which he was confronted, and also the capacity to draw connections between subjects that remained obscure to the more conventionally trained. The letters of this volume leave open to what extent Mileva could draw on similar resources when she took up her studies at the ETH. But they do suggest that she faced exams with less nonchalance than did Einstein, and that, while more pedantic in her studies, she may have been less independent in assimilating the received physics tradition.

If readers do not limit themselves to a search for isolated evidence of Einstein's later accomplishments in the correspondence presented here, they have a unique chance of gaining glimpses into Einstein's thinking process, into the way he would elaborate ideas that he took from the literature, from his courses, or, as we shall see below, possibly even from an Aarau physics teacher. It is not that striking hints at later developments are entirely absent from the correspondence. When Einstein in 1901 is overcome by happiness and joy—which he naturally wants to share with Mileva—after reading a paper by Lenard on the generation of cathode rays by ultraviolet light (Letter 36), a historian of science cannot avoid thinking of Einstein's explanation of the photoelectric effect in 1905 that earned him a Nobel Prize seventeen years later. But one should avoid drawing hasty conclusions from such anticipations, which ignore the shifting contexts in his research. Very briefly, let us look at examples of what we mean.

The turn of the century was an exciting time for the development of physics, with new phenomena related to cathode rays, X rays, or radioactivity discovered year after year. The dispute over whether cathode rays are particles or waves was, in the late 1890s, increasingly decided in favor of the particle view. For X rays, on the other hand, the question of their nature was still open. Röntgen argued that they are longitudinal waves, but this was far from universally accepted. Einstein's letters to Mileva show that he did not stand as aloof from these recent developments of physics as is often argued. Already in 1899 he collaborated with one of the pioneers of X-ray research in Switzerland, an Aarau physics teacher, Conrad Wüest, with whom he conducted radiation experiments. For many years thereafter Einstein attentively followed X-ray research but did not publish on the subject. In his light-quantum paper of 1905, he proposes a surprising explanation of the photoelectric effect by assuming that, under certain circumstances, light behaves like particles. It may well be that this unorthodox idea first demonstrated its value to him in the entirely different context of research on X rays, where similar hypotheses were part of the contemporary debate. It thus appears reasonable to assume that some of Einstein pioneering contributions emerged from attempts to solve now-forgotten problems, and that in so doing, he developed conceptual tools applicable to other more prominent riddles. A perhaps even more striking illustration of this serendipitous character of scientific discovery is Einstein's search for a theory of thermoelectricity. The letters to Mileva not only amply document his now-forgotten passion for the subject, but also contain the unexpected revelation that his better-known contributions to statistical physics—indispensable tools for his later exploration of the quantum puzzle—were embedded in this previously unknown context of research.

The ideas documented by Einstein's letters could forever have remained only the half-baked projects of a brilliant adolescent. At the age of sixteen, already convinced that he had the requisite talent, he expressed a desire to become a theoretical scientist. But at times during his study at the ETH he seriously entertained the possibility of taking over his father's business. He accompanied Hermann Einstein on a trip through northern Italy to visit electric power plants set up by his father's firm, and Einstein junior described this trip in half-serious fashion, as a sacramental ritual for entering the family enterprise (Letter 18). At the ETH he took courses in business and banking, as well as in insurance statistics. As it turned out, Einstein was fortunate enough to be able to apply his knowledge of statistics to the explanation of the laws of Brownian motion rather than to the fluctuations of life and death statistics as summarized in the tables of an insurance firm.

Einstein also entertained other professional options, among them teaching and work at a patent office. His study at the ETH prepared him for a secondary-school teaching position, which would allow him to follow in the footsteps of the teachers he admired. He apparently liked teaching and he also knew how to make a living at it. Throughout his student years he gave private lessons, and after obtaining his diploma he worked as a substitute teacher in mathematics at a technical school in Winterthur, and later as teacher at a boarding school in Schaffhausen. When in July 1901 he learned that Mileva was pregnant, he promised to forgo all scientific and professional ambitions, and accept the lowliest position if necessary, in order to marry her. At that time, his highest ambitions seemed thwarted not only by his fiancée's pregnancy, but also because he had just received a devastating reply to his criticisms of Drude's electron theory. But Mileva's concern that he might throw away his talent to assume an unacceptable position just to make her happy was unnecessary: we note that Albert was able to draw on larger reserves of self-confidence and to continue to pursue his plans for a career in science.

By contrast, Mileva never had the luxury of choosing between the conventional path of teacher and more lofty ambitions. Already three months pregnant, she failed in her second attempt to obtain her teacher's certificate, and concerns for her future family and for the ups and downs of Albert's search for a position now increasingly overshadowed her own professional desires. In the end she apparently agreed to give up the illegitimate Lieserl and resigned herself to having a second child after their marriage. The available evidence suggests that by 1902 Mileva had ceased to be the intellectually and emotionally formidable partner Albert first began courting in Zurich five years earlier.

This does not, however, mean that intellectual partnership had become any less important for him. Already in the time of his correspondence with Mileva, Michele Besso emerges as a friend with whom Einstein could exchange ideas on science in freewheeling discussions. In his early Bern period, Einstein established a discussion group, which he mockingly called the Olympia Academy, with a pair of other bohemian friends. It would be unfair to dismiss Einstein's discussion partners as his "sounding boards," a characterization that Besso rejected outright. It was Besso, after all, who had originally called Mach's work to Einstein's attention and who had passed on the fund of applied thermodynamics he had acquired while an engineering student at the ETH. The same Besso pointed out to his friend in 1905 that the kind of molecular movement, whose laws Einstein had just theoretically derived, had already been observed earlier and was called "Brownian motion" by physiologists. And it is to his friend Michele Besso that Einstein dedicated the only acknowledgment in his relativity paper, a paper that stands out for its lack of any reference to the literature. The fact that Besso, like so many of Einstein's later discussion partners, was not a phys-

icist may have helped Einstein not only to escape the narrow dog-
matism of some fields in contemporary physics, but also to broaden
his horizons. Einstein cherished both the fruitful dilettantism of
Besso and his colleagues in the Olympia Academy and the bohemian cameraderie that they and Mileva granted him. Still, the correspondence that shows him and his band of outsiders united against
the rest of the world also hints at a deeper truth. Einstein acquired
a greater intellectual distance from the bohemian life than his letters
at first glance reveal. The bohemian life with Mileva and the bourgeois life with his parents, it seems, were only roles, from which
Einstein maintained an inner distance.

The philosophy of Schopenhauer, references to which are oc-
casionally seeded in the Einstein letters from this period, may have
provided him with a vocabulary that enabled him to deal with
conflicting loyalties and his ambivalent reactions to them—the frus-
tration at what he perceived to be the mindless life of his parents,
and yet his dependence on them; his love for Mileva, and yet his
feeling of claustrophobia in the little world they had made for themselves; his love for the higher values of science, and yet the sometimes humiliating need of having to struggle to make a scientific
career. Schopenhauer would also have struck other sympathetic
chords in him, such as his praise of music as the one pleasure in
which the solitary genius can find himself, and his biting observations of other people's weaknesses. It is, after all, Schopenhauer's
portrait of the lonely intellectual that provided a whole generation
of educated Germans with a powerful identification, in opposition to
the excessively materialistic society of Wilhelmine Germany.

In his aphorisms Schopenhauer defines the philistine—a recur-
ring theme in Einstein's correspondences—as a man without intellectual needs, and situates him against the "genius" whose role is
to lead the blind masses to higher development by merely living
among them. Taking distance from these masses, Schopenhauer re-
garded bourgeois marriage with contempt and saw little difference
between wife and prostitute, a view that Einstein expresses in Letter
16. Perhaps even more important is another aspect of this philosophy that also finds Einstein's sympathy: Schopenhauer formulates a

protest against philistine life that permits those who can identify with the "genius" of his writings to continue to live as philistines so long as they do not surrender their inner being to such an existence as well.

A cursory examination cannot nearly exhaust the themes touched on in Mileva's and Albert's letters. There is also, for instance, Einstein's little-known interest in psychology which may have been related to epistemological questions but which, like his reading of Schopenhauer, may also have offered him a vocabulary for reflecting on his emotions. This interest was shared if not stimulated by Mileva's concern for the physiological and ethical limits of human thinking, evident from several of her letters. To the extent that the fragmentary character of what has remained permits such a conclusion, it even seems that psychology was of greater interest to her than physics. But any attempt to assess Mileva's interest in physics and the ideas she developed in discussion with Albert risks failure for the same reasons that silenced her voice in the letters she wrote: they were discarded, and with them the memory of her possible contributions. Since we cannot replace by speculation what has been lost in evidence, let us return to the question posed at the beginning of this introduction: How was a young man able to see the conceptual implications in the works of such masters as Lorentz and Planck that they themselves were unable to discern? Einstein was confronted with their results as an outsider, free to interpret them in his own way, and not as an adherent of an established school of thinking from which he would have inherited a more or less comprehensive but closed view of science. Being a nonspecialist in this sense, he was, however, also a young man who could rely on unusual resources of knowledge and experience. This in turn allowed him to impart new meaning to the work of the masters, each of whose achievements was technically sophisticated and might have absorbed the full attention of a disciple. But as a wanderer between the worlds, as a bourgeois and as a bohemian, as an atomist and as a critic of atomism, Einstein was able to partake of the insights and emotions of a variety of worlds and yet yield to none of them.

Jürgen Renn and Robert Schulmann

Textual Note

🐦

Letters 1 through 51 were originally published in *The Collected Papers of Albert Einstein* (*CPAE* throughout this edition), Vol. 1 (Princeton, N.J.: Princeton University Press, 1987). The last three letters have not appeared previously, and are scheduled for publication in 1993 in Vol. 5 of *CPAE*.

The annotation in this volume has been slightly modified from the editorial material in *CPAE*, Vol. 1, and the forthcoming Vol. 5, which should be consulted if details regarding archival and administrative sources are needed. References to documents in *CPAE* other than those presented here are indicated by volume and document number.

Physical descriptions of the letters, and the original German texts, are available in *CPAE*, Vol. 1, and the forthcoming Vol. 5. Where dates are provided in brackets, but not explained by a footnote, the information is taken from a postmark on a postcard or envelope. In cases where a letter appears without salutation or closure, or both, the source is an incomplete draft of a letter or a textual fragment.

Translator's Note

It should be noted that Einstein and Marić address each other with the formal "Sie" form in German until Letter 13, the first letter in which the familiar "Du" is used. The difference is similar to that of the now archaic formal "you" and familiar "thou" distinction in English.

In the early letters, both Einstein and Marić use initials in salutations, indicating a certain stage in their developing intimacy. I have expanded such cases.

I have retained a few German terms that do not have English equivalents. An *Assistent* (plural *Assistenten*) assists a professor in his teaching, laboratory, and research duties, often while working to obtain a doctorate or a position as a *Privatdozent* (unpaid university lecturer). Some *Privatdozenten* double as *Assistenten*. The *Diplom* is roughly equivalent to the baccalaureate and its acquisition requires the completion of a thesis, the *Diplomarbeit*. The holder of a *Diplom* can teach his or her subject in a secondary school or be eligible for a professional position in business or industry.

Any untranslatable plays on words by Einstein are explained in the notes.

Shawn Smith

Albert Einstein

Mileva Marić

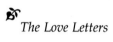

The Love Letters

1 *Marić to Einstein*

🐦

[Heidelberg, after 20 October 1897][1]

It's been quite a while since I received your letter, and I would have answered immediately to thank you for your sacrifice in writing a four-page letter, thus repaying a bit of the enjoyment you gave me during our hike together—but you said I shouldn't write until I was bored—and I am very obedient (just ask Fräulein Bächtold).[2] I waited and waited for boredom to set in, but until today my waiting has been in vain, and I'm not sure what to do about it. On the one hand, I could wait until the end of time, but then you would think me a barbarian—on the other, I still can't write you with a clear conscience.

As you've already heard, I've been walking around under German oaks in the lovely Neckar valley,[3] whose allure is unfortunately now bashfully cloaked in a thick fog. No matter how much I strain my eyes, that's all I see; it's as desolate and gray as infinity.

I don't think the structure of the human skull is to be blamed for man's inability to understand the concept of infinity. He would certainly be able to understand it if, when young, and while developing his sense of perception, he were allowed to venture out into the universe rather than being cooped up on earth or, worse yet, confined within four walls in a provincial backwater. If someone can conceive of infinite happiness, he should be able to comprehend the infinity of space—I should think it much easier. And human beings are so clever and have accomplished so much, as I have observed once again here in the case of the Heidelberg professors.

Papa[4] gave me some tobacco that I'm to give you personally. He's eager to whet your appetite for our little land of outlaws. I told him all about you—you absolutely must come back with me someday—the two of you would really have a lot to talk about! But I'll have to play the role of interpreter. I can't send the tobacco, however, because should you have to pay duty on it, you would curse me *and* my present.

Is it Herr Sänger who's become a forester?[5] The poor fellow probably wants to smother his love in a highly romantic Swiss forest. But it serves him right; what's the point of him falling in love nowadays anyway? It's such an old story how much human beings think they know. You could sit and listen to them for the rest of your life and they would still be regaling you with all that they have discovered. It really was too enjoyable in Prof. Lenard's lecture yesterday;[6] now he's talking about the kinetic theory of gases.[7] It seems that oxygen molecules travel at a speed of over 400 m per second,[8] and after calculating and calculating, the good professor set up equations, differentiated, integrated, substituted, and finally showed that the molecules in question actually do move at such a velocity, but that they only travel the distance of 1/100 of a hair's breadth.

2   *Einstein to Marić*

Zurich, Wednesday [16 February 1898]

Dear Fräulein,

The desire to write you has finally conquered the guilty conscience I've had about not responding to your letter for such a long time, and which has allowed me to avoid your critical eye. But now, even though you are understandably angry with me, you must at least give me credit for not adding to my offense by hiding behind feeble excuses, and for asking you simply and directly for forgiveness and—for an answer as soon as possible.

I'm glad that you intend to return here to continue your studies. Come back soon; I'm sure you won't regret your decision.[1] I am convinced that you will be able to catch up rather quickly on our most important course work. Still, it's most embarrassing for me to have to recount the material we've covered. Only here will you find the material properly organized and explained.

Hurwitz lectured on differential equations, except for partials, as well as Fourier series, and some on the calculus of variations and double integrals.[2] Herzog spoke very clearly and well on the strength of materials, and somewhat superficially on dynamics, but that's to be expected in a "mass course."[3] Weber lectured masterfully on heat (temperature, heat quantities, thermal motion, dynamic theory of gases). I eagerly anticipate every class of his. Fiedler is lecturing on projective geometry; he's the same indelicate rough person he always was, and a little impenetrable at that, though he's always brilliant and profound. In short: a master but unfortunately a terrible pedant too. The only other important course that will give you much to do is number theory, but you can make it up gradually by studying on your own.[4]

If you don't mind my giving you some advice (entirely unselfishly?), you should return as soon as possible, because everything you need to catch up on your studies can be found tightly packed in our notebooks.[5] To be on the safe side, you might want to write Hurwitz beforehand to clear it with him.[6] I don't think you'll have any trouble in the short or long term in getting a room at the Bächtolds again, as they have one room which is not rented definitely.[7] You will, of course, have to give up your old pleasant room which a Zurich philistine now occupies . . . serves you right, you little runaway!

But now back to the books. Best wishes, your

Albert Einstein

3   Einstein to Marić

𝔟

[Zurich, after 16 April 1898][1]

Dear Fräulein,

When I came home just now, I found the apartment locked with no one at home, and had to beat a shameful retreat. So, don't be angry with me for taking Drude[2] in this emergency in order to do some studying.

Best wishes from your   Albert Einstein

4   Einstein to Marić

𝔟

[Zurich, after 16 April 1898][1]

D[ear] F[räulein] M[arić],

Please don't be angry with me for keeping to myself so long. I was seriously ill, so much so that I didn't dare leave my room. Even today my legs are still a little weak. Nevertheless, this afternoon I gathered up my courage and ventured out for a stroll. I told Frau Bächtold to invite any of her boarders who feel like it for a get-together, and I hope you are among those who come. But if you can't make it, I'll visit you as soon as I feel well enough. And if I'm not able to go out, I'll look forward to your visit soon.

With best wishes, your   Albert Einstein

I've read half of the tome already.[2] I find it stimulating and informative, though the specifics sometimes lack clarity and precision.

5 *Einstein to Marić*

[Zurich, after 28 November 1898][1]

Dear Fräulein,

Marco Besso died Sunday night.[2] A terrible blow for his family, but better than a miserable life.

If you don't mind, I'd like to come over this evening to read with you. Your   Albert Einstein

6 *Einstein to Marić*

[Milan] Monday [13 or 20 March 1899][1]

Dear [Saud?],

You came vividly to mind during a harsh scolding I just received. This little letter will serve as proof that I thought of you.

To the paragon I give a sample (worthless of course).[2] Has it arrived yet? If not, then don't give me such a smug smile. It's not meant to be eaten. Oh yes—the letter for the paragon will be put inside the sample in emulation of famous examples[3]—acting boldly is half the battle.

I'm having a wonderful time at home; I've spent much of it tending to the innermost joys, that is to say, I've been eating a lot, and well, something which has already caused me to suffer a bit from our favorite poetic ailment, like the time at the Sterns[4] when for hours I sat next to you, my charming table partner. It was then revealed to me in harsh tints how closely knit our psychic and physiological lives are.

The journey was very pleasant, despite the fact unfortunately that my companions in the compartment were all males. There were a couple of frisky Italian boys who sang and laughed and joked with each other, sounding half like little girls, half like puppies. Things went well in Chiasso.[5] "This fellow doesn't have anything of interest," the sly customs officer must have thought to himself. I spent the rest of the journey in deep conversation with a young man about Italian affairs, while a young German salesman on his first trip to Italy took great pains to show off the few Italian expressions he had acquired for just such an occasion with as much elegance and nonchalance as possible. It was as if someone with a trumpet that only played two notes wanted to perform in an orchestra and was continually waiting—continually longing for the next chance to blow his horn.

Your photograph had quite an effect on my old lady.[6] While she studied it carefully, I said with the deepest sympathy: "Yes, yes, she certainly is a clever one." I've already had to endure much teasing about this, among other things, but I don't find it at all unpleasant.

My musings on radiation are beginning to take on more substance—I myself am curious if anything will come of it.

Best wishes *etc.*, especially the latter, from your   Albert

My old lady sends her best.

7 Einstein to Marić

🐦

Paradise [Mettmenstetten, early August 1899][1]

D[ear] D[ollie],

You must really be surprised to see my hieroglyphics again so soon, especially since you know how lazy I am when it comes to writing letters.

Here in Paradise[2] I live a nice, quiet, philistine life with my mother hen and sister[3]—it's just as the pious and the upright imagine paradise to be. In my spare time I've studied quite a bit of Helmholtz on atmospheric movements[4]—but out of my fear of you (as well as for my own pleasure), I hasten to add that I promise to reread it with you later. I admire the originality and independence of Helmholtz's thought more and more. You, poor girl, must now stuff your head with gray theory,[5] but I know that with your divine composure, you'll accomplish everything with a level head. Besides, you are at home being pampered, as a deserving daughter should be. But in Zurich you are the mistress of our house, which isn't such a bad thing, especially since it's such a nice household! When I read Helmholtz for the first time I could not—and still cannot—believe that I was doing so without you sitting next to me. I enjoy working together very much, and find it soothing and less boring.

My mother and sister seem somewhat petty and philistine to me, despite the sympathy I feel for them. It is interesting how gradually our life changes us in the very subtleties of our soul, so that even the closest of family ties dwindle into habitual friendship. Deep inside we no longer understand one another, and are incapable of actively empathizing with the other, or knowing what emotions move the other.

Now you have a little something to decipher, but only a little, because you can devote only a short time to me now. If you get a chance, write me again, but if not, I'll know the reason.

Best wishes to your family, and especially to you, from your

Albert

8 *Einstein to Marić*

Paradise [Mettmenstetten] Thursday [10? August 1899][1]

D[ear] D[ollie],

Many thanks for your letter. I would have replied sooner but I went on a hike through the mountains with the owner of our hotel[2]—it was wonderful, by the way (Zug-Einsiedeln[3]–Upper Lake of Zurich). I hope you received my first letter, even though it contained little of importance, because otherwise you would most certainly harbor bitter resentment toward me and consider me an unfaithful lazybones. The vacation offers me peace and quiet, so it is the studying that is a welcome diversion for me, not the loafing—just the opposite of the situation in our household. And you, good soul, write me that cramming agrees with you—that's what I like to hear. You're such a robust girl and have so much vitality in your little body. I returned the Helmholtz volume[4] and am now rereading Hertz's propagation of electric force[5] with great care because I didn't understand Helmholtz's treatise on the principle of least action in electrodynamics.[6] I'm convinced more and more that the electrodynamics of moving bodies as it is presented today doesn't correspond to reality,[7] and that it will be possible to present it in a simpler way. The introduction of the term "ether" into theories of electricity has led to the conception of a medium whose motion can be described, without, I believe, being able to ascribe physical meaning to it.[8] I think that electrical forces can be directly defined only for empty space, something also emphasized by Hertz.[9] Further, electrical currents will have to be thought of not as "the disappearance of electrical polarization over time," but as the motion of true electrical masses whose physical reality appears to be confirmed by electrochemical equivalents.[10] Mathematically they can then always be understood in the form $\frac{\partial X}{\partial x} + . + .$ [11] Electrodynamics would then be the theory of the movements of moving electricities and magnetisms[12] in empty space: which of the two views prevails depends on the results of the radiation experiments.—By the way, I haven't heard anything from Rector Wüest yet.[13] I'll write to him soon.

Here in Paradise it is always very beautiful, especially since we have such wonderful weather. We are always having unpleasant visits from Mother's acquaintances though. I can usually manage to escape their mindless prattle by slipping away if we don't happen to be at the dinner table. At the end of our stay my aunt from Genoa is coming,[14] a veritable monster of arrogance and insensitive formalism. I'm nevertheless enjoying each and every day of my vacation in this wonderfully peaceful place. If only you could be here with me for a while! We understand one another's dark souls so well, and also drinking coffee and eating sausages etc. . . .

You're probably right that I only imagined the story about you and Mama. It certainly never would have occurred to you. Make sure you write me here next time. You must have misunderstood me earlier. I always enjoy reading your little lines; send me some more again soon.

Best wishes from your   Albert

Don't work too hard!
Best wishes from Mama and Maja!

Best wishes to your family.
Greetings, P. Einstein[15]
I would have liked to write you too, but A. wouldn't let me. M.[16]

9 *Marić to Einstein*

🐦

[Kać, after 10 August–before 10 September 1899][1]

D[ear] H[err] E[instein],

Both of your letters[2] have found me contented at our country retreat;[3] I thank you for them, and look forward to receiving another one soon. I certainly hope that you, who have so much time on your hands, don't follow my example just now that I'm writing somewhat less. Your every letter gives me warm memories of home. Our series of shared experiences has secretly given me a strange feeling that is evoked at the slightest touch, without necessarily conjuring up the memory of a particular moment, and makes me feel, so it seems, as if I were in my room once again.

You're right not to study much, if only it were true. That your country life is completely peaceful is hard to believe; you'd better enjoy some pleasant walks while you can. The entire time I've been home I've gotten no farther than the garden. We don't go into town at all now because many cases of scarlet fever and diphtheria have been reported. We prefer to remain here in our fresh, healthy air. Novi Sad is a very unhealthy place these days, in addition to being so terribly hot. Our sour cherry trees are blooming for the second time.

Give my best wishes to Frau Einstein and Fräulein Maja; I would be happy to receive a letter from her (that is, of course, with your permission; I don't understand why not, unless you really have a good reason). The "cramming" proceeds slowly. Fiedler is my biggest headache and the material is the hardest to master.[4] Perhaps you could write me a little about what to expect on the exam, but don't think that this means you're excused from including things other than a report (just in case). Do Fiedler and Herzog[5] ask for specific things, examples, or do they ask only general questions? Can I also ask you to leave your notebook on heat theory with Frau

Markwalder[6] when you get back to Zurich; I want to look up a few things.

You don't say in your letter when you're leaving Paradise. I'll probably be back in Zurich on the 25th, but rather than looking forward to it, I'm returning with mixed feelings. Don't you feel sorry for me?[7]

I hope you're not letting anyone read my letters; you must give me your word. You said once you don't like disrespect, and if I feel that this is being disrespectful, you can do it for me! What do you think? I'll address you differently the next time I write. I've thought of a nicer way (it is very pious), but it occurred to me too late.—

You must excuse me if my scribbling shows signs of absentmindedness. I seem to have picked up a slight case of it, but not for long I hope.

Best wishes, and write again soon to your   D[ollie]

10 *Einstein to Marić*

Sunday, Paradise [Mettmenstetten, 10 September 1899][1]

D[ear] D[ollie],

I can finally write to acknowledge your dear little letter.[2] I wish I could have answered it the very day it came, but it had to be forwarded to me in Aarau, where it is so lovely that one is easily distracted, and I find it impossible to write.

You poor thing, you must be working so terribly hard! I wish there were something I could do to help, if only by adding some variety to your life or to your studies, or by being your Johnnie, with all the nice odds and ends appended.

All of this will soon be behind you and you can chalk it up as yet another success when you receive that important little piece of white paper. I was pressed for time while in Zurich yesterday and didn't get a chance to take the physics notebook to your apartment. Don't pout about it, you little witch! When you get back to Zurich just go up to my room and take whatever you like. If you can't find what you're looking for, ask Frau Markwalder (she knows everything, doesn't she?). —The day after tomorrow I'm off to Milan with my mother and won't be back to "our place" in Zurich until the beginning of the semester. I would so much like to be in Zurich to make your exam period more pleasant, but that would understandably cause my parents a great deal of pain.

At present, I'm completely bookless for a week while various libraries are taking inventory,[3] but within a week I can have the municipal library send books by Helmholtz, Boltzmann, and Mach[4] to me in Milan. So you don't fret and frown about it, I solemnly promise to go over everything again with you. I think we should stay in Zurich for the holidays some time, so we can enjoy college life without lectures for a change; what a pleasure that would be.

In Aarau I had a good idea for investigating the way in which a body's relative motion with respect to the luminiferous ether affects the velocity of the propagation of light in transparent bodies.[5] I even came up with a theory about it that seems quite plausible to me. But enough of this! Your poor little head is already crammed full of other people's hobby horses that you've had to ride. I won't bother you with mine as well. I can't think of any other assurances to offer you, other than to say that you shouldn't let this little exam bother you too much. That should be easy for you—especially with such harmless competition.

Take care of yourself, don't work too hard, accept my thousand warmest wishes, and address me more nicely in your next letter. Your   Albert
                                                                    Via Biglia 21
                                                                    Milano

Best wishes to your family
      "   "   from Mama and Maja.

11   *Einstein to Marić*

🐚

D[ear] D[ollie],

It was nice of you, you sweet girl, to write me when you have so much strenuous work to do. But you should also know that your letters make me so happy that everyone teases me about it. You must have had to swallow a lot of book dust recently, you poor thing, but it will soon be over—I know how you feel. I've been quite a bookworm myself lately, trying to work out several ideas, some of them very interesting. I also wrote to Professor Wien in Aachen[2] about my paper on the relative motion of the luminiferous ether against ponderable matter, the paper which the "boss" handled in such an offhanded fashion.[3] I read a very interesting paper by Wien from 1898 on this subject.[4] He'll write me via the Polytechnic (if it's certain!). If you see a letter for me there you can go ahead and open it.

I'll be back at "our place" around the 15th. I'm really looking forward to returning because it's still the nicest and coziest place I can think of. Maja is going to Aarau mainly because we know a family there quite well,[5] and also because it's much cheaper to live there—we must be on our guard.

Frau Markwalder feels obliged to . . . . She is an angel of foresight. I already wrote her that I agreed, and gave her permission to rent the room to whomever she liked. I'll move somewhere on Plattenstrasse, but not into your house—we don't want to start any rumors.[6] I'd like to move to the Zürichberg, and would if it weren't so far from "our place."

The fiddling should be behind you by the time you get this letter[7]—I've been thinking about it so much lately. I'm sure everything will go well—your hard little head assures me of that. If only I could look through the keyhole! When taking such an examination you feel so responsible for everything you think and do that it's as if you were in a prison. Don't you think so? Grossmann and I laughed a lot about these things when we were preparing for the exam[8]—but impartially one might say: "Laughing on the outside while crying on the inside."

My sister probably won't spend any time in Zurich at all, and after accompanying her to Aarau I'll come right back. I'm starting to feel uneasy here; the climate doesn't suit me, and without anything in particular to work on I tend to brood a lot—in short, I'm beginning to feel the absence of your beneficent thumb, under which I'm always kept in line.

Neuweiler is the dark fellow who always drinks milk.[9] He also wears glasses and is rather scrawny. Don't worry about my going to Aarau so often now that the critical daughter with whom I was so madly in love four years ago is coming back home.[10] For the most part, I feel quite secure in my high fortress of calm. But I know that if I saw her a few more times I would certainly go mad. Of that I am certain, and I fear it like fire.

When I'm back in Zurich, the first thing we'll do is climb the Ütliberg.[11] There we can take pleasure in unpacking our memories of the Säntis;[12] I can already imagine the fun we'll have. And then we'll start in on Helmholtz's electromagnetic theory of light,[13] which I still haven't read—(1) because I'm afraid to, and (2) because I didn't have it.

A thousand warm wishes from your   Albert

12 *Einstein to Marić*

🖎

Milan, Tuesday [10 October 1899][1]

D[ear] S[weet] D[ollie],

Now that's a fine way to behave! You've already been comfortably taking your exams for four days now and I, your good colleague and fellow coffee-guzzler, have yet to hear so much as a peep out of you. Isn't that shocking? I'll have to rehearse a stern sermon for when I see you next Monday—it will be held as early as possible. And if the girl at the door says that you've gone out and I see your shiny little boots in front of the door—as sometimes happens—then I'll just wait a bit more or go get a shave.

I'm taking my sister to Aarau on Sunday and will arrive at my dear ex-landlady's house in Zurich the very same day.[2] She simply hasn't answered the postcard in which I dared to ask if it was within her "infinite capacity for foresight" to find me lodgings somewhere else. In other words, I, the poor little parcel, must wait for delivery until someone finds me an address. When I think how you must now be buried in work, my anger about your not writing me melts away like wax. You poor thing, you've really had it a lot harder than I had it in the last year, being so alone and all. But wait—I can already see you smiling at my attempts at consolation, and thinking: such things are of little concern to Dollie; she knows what she wants and has demonstrated this frequently.

But now for something more pleasant—I'm thinking of our household, of course. It will certainly be as nice a place as before. I'm bringing a few luscious goodies from Mama, who promised to send us something for the household every so often: directly to Plattenstrasse 50.[3] Pick up a copy of Helmholtz's electromagnetic theory of light in the meantime![4] I already crave it quite a bit.

I have done a lot of studying here and have completed my deliberations on the fundamental laws of thermoelectricity.[5] I have also come up with a very simple method of determining whether the latent heat of metals[6] can be reduced to the motion of ponderable matter or of electricity, i.e., whether an electrically charged body has a different specific heat from an uncharged one.[7] All of these questions are related to the analysis of the thermoelement. The procedures can be carried out very simply and require no equipment that is not readily available to us.[8]

That's enough for today; any more and my parents will tease me for writing so much without first getting a reply. Best wishes, and looking forward to a happy reunion, your   Albert

13 *Marić to Einstein*

ℬ

[1900?][1]

My dear Johnnie,

Because I like you so much, and because you're so far away that I can't give you a little kiss, I'm writing this letter to ask if you like me as much as I do you? Answer me *immediately*.

A thousand kissies from your   Dollie

ஐ

My dearest Dollie,

> Because I'm writing in my bed,
> This letter is with labor read!
> But I scribble on without a rest
> So Dollie may read with interest! . . . .

I arrived in Sarnen the day before yesterday[2] as planned, with the dreadful aunt in tow. We were met by Mama, Maja, and a carriage.[3] At this point I was smothered with kisses. Then we drove off, but after a while Maja and I got off to walk. Maja took this opportunity to say that she had not dared to mention anything about the "Dollie affair," and asked me to "go easy" on Mama—that is to say—to keep my big mouth shut.

So we arrive home,[4] and I go into Mama's room (only the two of us). First I must tell her about the exam,[5] and then she asks me quite innocently: "So, what will become of your Dollie now?" "My wife," I said just as innocently, prepared for the proper "scene" that immediately followed. Mama threw herself onto the bed, buried her head in the pillow, and wept like a child. After regaining her composure she immediately shifted to a desperate attack: "You are ruining your future and destroying your opportunities." "No decent family will have her." "If she gets pregnant you'll really be in a mess." With this last outburst, which was preceded by many others, I finally lost my patience. I vehemently denied that we had been living in sin and scolded her roundly, and was about to leave the room when Mama's friend Frau Bär came in.[6] She is a small, vivacious lady: an old hen of the most pleasant variety. We immediately began talking about the weather, the new guests at the spa, the ill-mannered children, etc. Then we ate, and afterwards played some music. When everyone had left, and the time came for Mama and me to say good night, it started all over again, but "*più piano*." The next day things were better, largely because, as she said herself: "If they have not yet been intimate (which she had greatly feared) and are willing to wait longer, then ways and means can always be found." The only thing that is embarrassing for her is that we want to remain together always. Her attempts at changing my mind came in expressions such as: "Like you, she is a book—but you ought to have a wife." "By the time you're 30 she'll be an old witch," etc. But now that she's seen that for the time being her efforts only make me angry, she's refrained from giving me the "treatment" for a while.

The people here and their way of life are hopelessly empty, and I completely understand Maja's dissatisfaction. She can hardly wait to get back to Aarau.[7] Each meal lasts one hour or more—you can imagine what hell that is for me. Due to the poor weather, I have in desperation taken refuge in Kirchhoff.[8] Besides those already mentioned, the hangers-on here include my aunt, the English lady, the Contessa, and her daughter, who is as beautiful as she is stupid and cold. For Mama's sake I must flatter and play music for all of them—otherwise she is offended, particularly since she is doubly sensitive because of the "affair."

If only I could be with you again soon in Zurich, my little treasure! A thousand wishes and the biggest kisses from your

Johnnie

"Kisses from Maja"
Don't write to our dear Weber any more; he'll be in the country.

15 *Einstein to Marić*

🐦

[Melchtal] Wednesday evening [1 August 1900][1]

My sweet little one,

I'm so happy to know that you're back home again with your old lady,[2] who is now fattening up my dear Dollie so she can rest in my arms healthy and happy once again, as plump as a dumpling. Think of it, you will be resting in your beloved *Oxistent's* arms; though I still have no news from Zurich,[3] the carefree life and good food here have produced high spirits and confidence. I just realized that I haven't been able to kiss you for an entire month, and I long for you so terribly much. No one as talented and industrious as my Dollie, with her skilled hands, is to be found in this entire anthill of a hotel. Mama-in-law has already more or less made up with me and is slowly resigning herself to the inevitable. She has already regained her good mood. I have also written to Papa;[4] he said he is sending a separate letter. He will certainly resist at first too, but it doesn't matter.

I long terribly for a letter from my beloved witch. I can hardly believe that we will be separated so much longer—only now do I see how madly in love with you I am! Indulge yourself completely so you will become a radiant little darling and as wild as a street urchin.

Melchtal is a wonderful little river valley formed by high, but not glaciated, mountains. Our hotel is a particularly excellent feeding establishment, but I feel uncomfortable among these indolent and pampered people. Especially when I see these overdressed, lazy women who are always complaining about things. It is then that I think proudly: "Johnnie, your Dollie is a different kind of girl." Brandenberger is also here with his *fiancée*, a young girl from Zurich whom I like very much.[5] Both of them are clearly swimming in bliss—they make a very nice couple.

Yesterday I was with Maja on a rather high mountain where we found many edelweiss. We had a spectacular view, especially of the huge glaciers of the Titlis.[6]

Toward the middle of August we'll visit Papa in Italy to spend some time in a more southerly clime. Before that I will go to Zurich to check on my position. I have no news from Ehrat either.[7] Because it rains a lot, I've been studying a good deal, mainly Kirchhoff's notorious investigations of the motion of the rigid body.[8] I can't stop marveling at this great work. My nerves have calmed down enough so that I'm able to work happily again. How are yours?

Best wishes to your dear family! Tender kisses from your

Albert

16 *Einstein to Marić*

[Melchtal] Monday [6 August 1900][1]

My dear little one,

Your first dear little letter from home arrived yesterday. I went off by myself to read the lines in silence, then twice more, and then I read between the lines with great joy for a long time before shoving the letter into my pocket and smiling to myself. "Mama-in-law" has been very pleasant and doesn't touch on the "delicate subject" anymore. Since I've been in a cheerful mood, and because my popularity among the guests here and my "musical successes" act as a balm on her wounded mother-in-law's heart, it is quite pleasant here now.

But our correspondence, darling, appears to have been cursed, as you had not received my letter by the time you sent yours. This is the third one I'm sending.[2]

I still haven't heard anything from Zurich. I guess I'll have to look into the situation myself. Considering Ehrat's conscientiousness, the only thing I can think of is that his position is still very much up in the air.

Take it easy, sweetheart, there will be plenty of time later for studying with your Johnnie. Have a good rest in the meantime and enjoy your carefree life.

Papa has written me a moralistic letter for the time being, and promised that the main part would be delivered in person soon. I'm looking forward to it dutifully. I understand my parents quite well. They think of a wife as a man's luxury, which he can afford only when he is making a comfortable living. I have a low opinion of this view of the relationship between man and wife, because it makes the wife and the prostitute distinguishable only insofar as the former is able to secure a lifelong contract from the man because of her more favorable social rank. Such a view follows naturally from the fact that in the case of my parents, as with most people, the senses exercise a direct control over the emotions. With us, thanks to the fortunate circumstances in which we live, the enjoyment of life is vastly broadened. But we mustn't forget how many existences like my parents' make our existence possible. In the social development of mankind, the former are a far more important constituency. Hunger and love are and remain such important mainsprings of life that almost everything can be explained by them, even if one disregards the other dominant themes. Thus I am trying to protect my parents without compromising anything that is important to me—and that means you, sweetheart!

If you haven't said anything to your parents about this yet, don't! I think this will be better for all parties concerned. Otherwise they might start having the same unnecessary worries and misgivings as my parents. But then you're a smart girl and know the best way to handle them.

When I'm not with you I feel as if I'm not whole. When I sit, I want to walk; when I walk, I'm looking forward to going home; when I'm amusing myself, I want to study; when I study, I can't sit still and concentrate; and when I go to sleep, I'm not satisfied with how I spent the day.

Enjoy yourself, sweetheart, with tender kisses from your

Albert

17 *Einstein to Marić*

ஃ

Zurich, Thursday [9? August 1900][1]

My dear sweetheart,

You must be surprised to see me popping up here again so soon! I'm using the first best excuse I've had to get away from my boring surroundings, even though my mother took it upon herself to observe the deepest silence about the "affair." She acted as if nothing had happened, giving me your letters herself, and not noticing when I wrote you—in short, she has given up on open warfare and will probably wait to let loose the big philistine guns when she is joined by Papa. He promised in his last letter to travel with me to Venice, which is close to one of our power plants.[2] I'd also like to learn a little bit about the administration of the business so I can take Papa's place in an emergency. He doesn't mention you anymore either. I would have done better, darling, if we had kept everything to ourselves and delayed telling my parents. But no harm done, sweetheart; Mama and Papa are phlegmatic types and have less stubbornness in their entire bodies than I have in my little finger.

Though my old Zurich makes me feel very much at home again, I still miss you, my dear little "right hand." I can go anywhere I want—but I belong nowhere, and I miss your two little arms and that glowing mouth full of tenderness and kisses. How sorry I felt

24

for those Catholic nuns in Melchtal![3] I'll send you the measurements of my little feet another time;[4] I don't want you to start knitting again. And in exchange for your henlike enthusiasm you'll get a big kiss. —But now to the *excuse*. The night before last I received a card from Ehrat, who wrote that he had proposed me for an assistant's position with the insurance office in which he is presently working. For an eight-hour day of mindless drudgery one gets eight francs. But I turned it down, thinking I could make better use of my vacation time. One must avoid such stultifying affairs. For the time being, I'll remain here to see how the matter turns out, and to straighten out my "business and political" affairs. Among Ehrat's competition is Matter, the selection of whom would leave the door wide open for me to take up the position with Hurwitz. So have courage, little witch! I can hardly wait to be able to hug you and squeeze you and live with you again. We'll happily get down to work right away, and money will be as plentiful as manure. And if it's nice next spring, we'll pick flowers in Melchtal.

Tender kisses from your   Albert

18 *Einstein to Marić*

Zurich, Tuesday [14? August 1900][1]

Dear little sweetheart,

Once again I've let a few lazy days slip by without accomplishing anything. You know, the kind of days when you sleep late because there's nothing important to do, then go out until the room has been made up, and then study until fatigue sets in. Then you loaf around for a while and half-heartedly look forward to dinner, listlessly contemplating highly philosophical questions while whistling a little . . . . How was I able to live alone before, my little everything? Without you I lack self-confidence, passion for work, and enjoyment of life—in short, without you, my life is no life.

I have even begun visiting people to keep myself busy. I went to see Frau Markwalder, who still shows the same languid kindness and sees everything in an amorphous fuddle; it's a good thing I don't live with her anymore. I also visited the innocent little girl, who is still one of the nicest and most spirited people we know here. She is now leaving for good, for a town in the canton of Thurgau. I also visited your landlady.[2] She said your suitcase had been removed quite a while ago. She asked if you wanted to keep the room, and would have made arrangements to keep it free. I turned the offer down for you ("What a tyrant!" you must be thinking).

I won't allow you to be gone any longer than the first days of October; that's just enough time. I'm leaving for Italy on Saturday to partake of the "holy sacraments" administered by my father,[3] but the valiant Swabian is not afraid.[4] I hope I don't become stale like that when I get old, then it's okay. Your parents are proof that people don't have to wind up this way—they must be wonderful. But don't tell them too much about me or they might get frightened. I would have been smarter to have kept my mouth shut. Why did I not take better to heart my slogan, *omnes tractandi sunt*? On the other hand, it will be all the nicer when we're together again in Zurich, increasing our knowledge over fragrant coffee! I'm glad that your mother feeds you well and that your sister teases you all the time— and I'm especially proud that you're longing for me!

Don't study too hard when your books come; rest instead, so you can become my old street urchin again. There is only one thing I ask of you, and that is to take care of yourself—if not, then I'll spank you. Ehrat still doesn't have the position in Frauenfeld. He's in competition with Matter. One of them will get it in any case. I'm provided for in any case. I could have taken a job in a life insurance company for three weeks at eight francs a day, but turned it down because I thought I could make better use of my vacation time by studying a few things of importance and by learning about my father's business in Italy. It is quite possible, after all, that he could suddenly take ill, or become otherwise indisposed, and he has no one else to turn to. How pleasant it will be next year!

With best wishes and tender kisses, the last especially, from your   Albert

19 *Einstein to Marić*

Milan, Monday [20 August 1900][1]

My dear little one,
Four quartets:

> Oh my! That Johnnie boy!
> So crazy with desire,
> While thinking of his Dollie,
> His pillow catches fire.

> When my sweetie mopes around the house
> I shrivel up so small,
> But she only shrugs her shoulders
> And doesn't care at all.

> To my folks all this
> Does seem a stupid thing,
> But they never say a single word
> For fear of Albert's sting!

> My little Dollie's little beak,
> It sings so sweet and fine;
> And afterwards I cheerfully
> Close its song with mine.

Darling, I've been here with the old folks for two days now and am very content with them. I've gotten none of the "treatment" at all. I haven't said much about you, but I drop your name every now and again. As far as I can tell, they have nothing against our relationship anymore—apparently because they no longer think we're ruining our future. They also realize that I won't let myself be influenced by anyone. If I don't provoke them, everything will take its merry course—we a happy young couple, and they satisfied and content with the arrangement.

Oh how happy I'll be to hold you close to my heart once again! It will be in the first days of October! But in the meantime you should enjoy yourself, my only sweet little woman. I haven't heard anything about the "position."[2] I'm taking it easy though. If I don't get it then the "whole family" will just have to give private lessons. Thanks to the good domestic feedings and my parents' good humor I have become much more optimistic. My father is a completely different man now that he has no more financial worries. You can tell that all the dark clouds have disappeared by the fact that he's going to Venice with me after we've visited his power plants. I'm so delighted I could kiss you, my dear little angel!

But you haven't written me in a long time, you wild witch! Are you afraid it will "miss its mark," or are you just mad at me, you little rascal? Or do you want me to wonder and hunger for you? Or are you afraid of sisterly teasing?

> From him she now does hide away,
> What should he make of this?
> To him she is with all her soul
> Devoted with a kiss.

But because you are such a terrible little rascal I'll stop, mad as the devil!

Greetings and kisses from your   Albert

20 *Einstein to Marić*

🖎

Milan, via Bigli 21. Thursday night in bed
[30 August or 6 September 1900][1]

My dear kitten,

Today I received your registered letter, from which I could tell you were afraid it might fall into someone else's hands. No, darling, I received all of your dear little letters on time, even the money you sent me in Melchtal a while ago. Feel free to write what's on your mind, because it would be as unwise as it would be useless for my parents to keep one of your letters from me. You shouldn't worry about such things because I don't think my parents are capable of behaving like that. I've already put Mama to the test. My parents are very worried about my love for you. Mama often cries bitterly and I don't have a single moment of peace here. My parents weep for me almost as if I had died. Again and again they complain that I have brought misfortune upon myself by my devotion to you, they think you aren't healthy . . . . Oh Dollie, it's enough to drive one mad! You wouldn't believe how I suffer when I see how much they both love me, and yet they are so inconsolable you would think I had committed the greatest crime, and had gone against what my heart and conscience told me was indisputably true. If only they knew you! But it's as if they're under a spell, thinking all the while that I am. On Saturday I'm going on the business trip with Papa, and then to Venice. I was so distraught that I didn't want to go with him; but this alarmed them so much that I became quite frightened.

I'll only be able to recover from this vacation gradually, by being in your arms—there are worse things in life than exams. Now I know. This is worse than any external problem.

My only diversion is studying, which I am pursuing with redoubled effort, and my only hope is you, my dear, faithful soul. Without the thought of you I would no longer want to live among this sorry herd of humans. But having you makes me proud, and

29

your love makes me happy. I will be doubly happy when I can press you close to my heart once again and see those loving eyes which shine for me alone, and kiss your sweet mouth which trembles blissfully for me alone.

Thank God that August has slipped away. Four more weeks and we'll be together again and can live to bring each other joy. But then I won't let you go away again so soon!

I've been spending many evenings at Michele's.[2] I like him a great deal because of his sharp mind and his simplicity. I also like Anna, and especially their little kid.[3] His house is simple and cozy, though some of the details lack taste.

Kissing you from the bottom of my heart, your

Sweetheart

Friday. Tomorrow we're going on our trip, but I'll be back in a week, so don't stop sending me your little letters. Luigi Ansbacher[4] might come to visit us.

On the investigation of the Thomson effect I have again resorted to a different technique which is similar to your method for determining the dependence of κ on T and which also presupposes such an investigation.[5] If only we could start tomorrow! We'll need to be on good terms with Weber at all costs, because he has the best-equipped laboratory.[6]

With tender kisses, your

Albert

How's your little throat?[7]

I'm investigating the following interesting question for Michele: how does the radiation of electric energy through space occur in the case of a sinusoidal alternating current? Concerning the amplitude of the waves produced as a function of the frequency of oscillation, etc.[8] . . . .

21   Einstein to Marić

𝕭

[Milan] Thursday [13? September 1900][1]

My dearest Dollie,

Three-quarters of our stupid time apart is now over. Soon I'll be with my sweetheart again and can kiss her, hug her, make coffee with her, scold her, study with her, laugh with her, walk with her, chat with her . . . . . + *ad infinitum*! We'll have another wonderful year together, don't you think? I've already announced that I'm staying with you for Christmas. I can't wait until I have you again, my everything, my little so-and-so, my street urchin, my little rascal! When I think of you now, for a second I don't want to anger or tease you ever again, only to be an angel all the time! What a nice illusion! But you'll still love me, won't you, even if I'm the same old rogue I've always been, full of whims and mischief, and as moody as ever!

I don't know if I've been writing to you as regularly as usual. But don't make angry faces about it—my aunt is visiting here (the famous one, from Genoa) with her little daughter, a sadly spoiled little brat.[2] There's no room at all for me to be alone to write you. And if I do it in front of my parents, they think I'm trying to spite them. They're being very nice to me, by the way, especially Papa; they seem to have reconciled themselves to the inevitable. I think they'll both come to like you very much once they get to know you. Now I'm happy that I told them everything. They should be happy too, because now that I've seen other people, I know that nowhere in the world would I be able to find someone better than you. But I also treasure you and want to give you the love you deserve. Even my work seems pointless and unnecessary if not for the thought that you are happy with what I am and what I do. I'm finally sending you the sketch of my gigantic little foot that I keep forgetting to send.

Johnnie's foot!

Since you have such a great imagination and are accustomed to astronomical distances, I think the adjoining work of art will suffice.

I'm glad you've been doing a lot of walking and have gotten a good sunburn—I can't wait to hug my little black girl! I'm also looking forward to working on our new papers. You must continue with your investigations—how proud I will be to have a little Ph.D. for a sweetheart, while I remain a completely ordinary person![3]

Didn't I mention in my last letter that Matter got the position in Frauenfeld?[4] This means that I'll become Hurwitz's servant, god-willing (because I'm a man, of course). It doesn't matter Dollie, at least it's *your* man!

The Boltzmann is absolutely magnificent.[5] I'm almost finished with it. He's a masterful writer. I am firmly convinced of the correctness of the principles of his theory, i.e., I am convinced that in the case of gases, we are really dealing with discrete mass points of definite finite size which move according to certain conditions. Boltzmann quite correctly emphasizes that the hypothetical forces between molecules are not an essential component of the theory, as the whole energy is essentially kinetic in character.[6] This is a step forward in the dynamic explanation of physical phenomena.

Do you also know that I've been shaving myself for quite some time now, and with great success? You'll see, Dollie! I can always do it while you're making coffee for lunch, so that I don't pound the books as usual while poor Dollie has to cook, and while lazy Johnnie lolls about after hastily obeying the rapidly uttered command: "grind this."

Best wishes and kisses, my sweetheart, and my best wishes to your family, from your   Albert

22 Einstein to Marić

ॐ

Zurich [Milan], Wednesday evening in bed
[19 September 1900][1]

My dear Dollie!

Thanks for your sweet letter and its nice dreams for the future, the noodles and the nagging, and also the plan to bring your fat little sister[2] along and introduce her to our "European culture." To impress her with it even more and to give her a high opinion of us as well, I've already bought two little coffee spoons for our household. What a joy it will be when I can hold you tight once again, my little street urchin, my little veranda, my everything!

Just think, early tomorrow I'm off to the mountains again—to climb a peak near the Lago Maggiore, and then to visit Isola Bella.[3] How nice it would be if Madame Federico Maier could also be there to marvel at the view, and then in the still of the night, sweetly to dispel my dark thoughts—right, sweet kitten! I can't wait to bite you and hug you when you're with me again—but now we must wait for more than three weeks because of that damned goiter. Is it any better? I plan on going to Zurich on October 1st to talk with Hurwitz personally about the position. It's certainly better than writing. Shall I look around for possible jobs for you? I think I'll try to find some private lessons that I could later turn over to you. Or do you have something else in mind? Write me about it!

No matter what happens, we'll have the most wonderful life in the world. Pleasant work and being together—and what's more, we now answer to no one, can stand on our own two feet, and enjoy our youth to the utmost. Who could have it any better? When we have scraped together enough money, we can buy bicycles and take a bike tour every couple of weeks. Your dear sister, whom I already know from her cheerful letters, will certainly enjoy being with us—I don't need to tell you that she's welcome—such a carefree, ornery little thing! While in a low mood yesterday I wrote to one of my favorite old teachers in Munich;[4] I wonder if he'll answer me.

I have already read the entire Boltzmann, and part of the spherical harmonics, which actually interest me a great deal now.[5] I suppose beggars can't be choosers . . . .

Luigi Ansbacher, about whom we always tease Maja, is coming in a few days—I'm looking forward to playing some music with him.

It had also already occurred to me that my sweetheart will be homeless when she gets to Zurich. Unfortunately, Mrs. Hägi[6] no longer has room in her new apartment, but I'll look around for something. Maybe I can find a room for both of you. If only I weren't afraid of the responsibility—I know what a spoiled brat you are.

Poor Helene has fallen in love, thanks to her beau's admirable persistence—her delicate spirit will now suffocate in his fat—a sad physiological prophecy.[7] It's really too bad about her. Moreover, I think that in a short time he'll be the same scoundrel he was before. Such a person doesn't readily change.

The "bridegroom" then, has become a veritable "husband"? You see, even in this age of skepticism, miracles do happen.

Best wishes to your family! But you I will kiss all over, wherever you'll let me, your   Johnnie

23 *Einstein to Marić*

ঙ

Milan, Wednesday [3 October 1900][1]

Dear Dollie,

I'm on the verge of having a terribly bad conscience about not having written you more lately, although I can't remember right off-hand when it was exactly that I wrote you last. Really, I shouldn't pester you anymore with the curtains now that we're about to see each other again soon, but your Johnnie is so dumb.

I'm glad that your sister is going to come after all. We'll knock some sense into her and drive away her homesickness, though I won't be able to do it in Serbian. So all that nagging has made things turn out all right after all! There's nothing like a female (but as a little scientist, you are naturally exempted from such character-izations).

I've extended my stay until early Sunday because I now enjoy it here so much. My parents have retreated, grudgingly and with hesitation, from the battle of Dollie—now that they have seen that they'll lose it. They enjoy themselves now in the beautiful weather and spare me further debate. Hurwitz still hasn't written me more, but I have hardly any doubt at all that I'll get the position.

Michele has already noticed that I like you, because even though I hardly ever mention you, when I told him I had to go to Zurich again, he said: "It looks like he wants to visit his little col-league; why else would he want to go to Zurich!" To that I said: "But unfortunately she's not there yet." I've been urging him to be-come a teacher, but I don't think he'll do it. Quite simply, he doesn't want himself and his family to be supported by his father,[2] but that's natural. It's too bad, because he is exceptionally intelligent.

I'm rather well versed in physical chemistry now.[3] I'm very enthusiastic about the accomplishments in this field over the last thirty years.[4] You'll enjoy it too when we go over it together. The methods of physical investigation used are also very interesting.

The most wonderful of all is the ion theory, which has proved itself magnificently in the most diverse areas.[5]

The results on capillarity I recently obtained in Zurich seem to be entirely new despite their simplicity. When we're back in Zurich we'll try to get some empirical data on this subject from Kleiner.[6] If this yields a law of nature, we'll send the results to Wiedemann's *Annalen*.[7]

The ex-bridegroom Fritz Winteler is visiting Anna now; he's a disgusting person who is unable to discuss anything outside his own field, and will be an *Assistent* again in Darmstadt.[8]

You don't like the philistine life anymore either, do you? He who has tasted freedom can no longer wear chains. I'm so lucky to have found you, a creature who is my equal, and who is as strong and independent as I am! I feel alone with everyone except you.

With tender kisses from your   Albert

Best wishes to your parents!
Dolderstr. 17[9]

24 *Einstein to Marić*

Milan, Saturday [23 March 1901][1]

My dear Dollie,

I'm surprised to see signs of life from you on the first day already. The situation with Riecke is pretty bad. I've more or less given up on the position.[2] I can't believe that Weber would let such a nice opportunity pass without meddling in things.[3] I've taken your advice, darling, and written Weber to let him know that he can't get away with doing such things behind my back. I also told him that I know my appointment depends entirely upon his recommendation. I'm really curious about what Ostwald will write.[4]

I came up with an interesting idea while returning to Italy. It seems to me that it is not out of the question that the latent kinetic energy of heat in solids and fluids can be thought of as the energy of electrical resonators.[5] If this is the case, then the specific heat and the absorption spectrum of solids would have to be related. The Dulong-Petit law would be valid for substances whose smallest parts show a certain total resonance in the electro-optical sense. Actually, all substances that satisfy the Dulong-Petit law are almost completely opaque and seem to exhibit nearly the same spectrum when heated.[6] On the other hand, organic substances which, as we have seen, have relatively low specific heats are all transparent and show continuous absorption spectra,[7] while, for example, mercury agrees quite nicely with the Dulong-Petit law and is completely opaque.[8] I'm almost convinced that the law is valid: Dulong's law is only satisfied in the case of opaque substances. Transparent substances always have a lower kinetic energy. Unfortunately, gases probably can't be used to solve this puzzle because of the ephemeral nature of gas-related phenomena. Compounds with high "internal" energy, however, do show bandlike absorption spectra.[9] What about the specific heat of glass with regard to its composition? It would have to have a lower molecular heat in comparison to the number of its molecules.[10] See if you can find some literature on this!

So what are you up to, my little devil? Make yourself some good coffee as often as you can and indulge yourself. I think about you a lot (without provocation) and still have pleasant memories of how happy you were on the last day we spent together. So let me take the opportunity to kiss your little mouth so as not to let the happiness pass!

Can you imagine all the things I left in Zurich! My nightshirt and wash things and toothbrush and comb and hairbrush. Send everything to my sister (Girls' School in Aarau) so she can bring them home with her.[11]

It's a good thing we didn't travel on the Axenstrasse.[12] It would have been a real mess. You couldn't even see the opposite shore.

I made the journey with a couple of young fellows. One of them actually studied mathematics and physics at Göttingen for four semesters! You can imagine how I interrogated him about what things are like there. We also discussed epistemology at length. He said that Riecke is a very friendly, jovial man, and as *Assistent* to him I would have very little to do . . . if, if . . . you know that little song we used to sing together so often.

I've hardly left the house at all since I've been back. I'm trying to lead a quiet life so as to calm my nerves a little. My parents are helping as much as possible; the poor things have been constantly aggravated and worried about the damned money. My dear uncle Rudolf ("The Rich") has been nagging them terribly.[13]

Get lots of work done, my love, and find yourself a friendly little room to enjoy yourself in. A little Ph.D. or professor kisses perfectly well too. Did you send a reprint to Wenger[14] too?

Best wishes and kisses from   Johnnie

25 *Einstein to Marić*

ॐ

Milan, Wednesday [27 March 1901][1]

My dear kitten,

Many thanks for your letters, and for all the true love contained therein. I kiss you and hug you with all my heart for it, just as you would want, and just as you deserve, darling. Riecke's rejection did not surprise me[2] and I'm absolutely convinced that Weber is to blame. The excuse is too improbable, and he doesn't mention the second position at all.[3]

I'm convinced that under these circumstances it doesn't make any sense to write to any more professors, because they'll surely turn to Weber for information about me at a certain point, and he'll just give me another bad recommendation. I'll turn to my former teachers in Aarau and Munich,[4] but above all I'll try to get a position as *Assistent* in Italy. To begin with, one of the main obstacles in getting a position doesn't exist here, namely anti-Semitism, which in German-speaking countries is as unpleasant as it is a hindrance.[5] And in the second place, I have very good connections here. Herr Ansbacher,[6] for example, is a close friend of the professor of chemistry at the local polytechnic,[7] and Michele's uncle is professor of mathematics.[8] It's true, Michele is an awful schlemiel, but I'll grab him by the collar and drag him to his uncle, where I'll do the talking myself. Michele is at his parents' house in Trieste right now with his wife and child and won't be back for about ten days. You don't have to worry about me saying anything to him or anyone else about you. You are and will remain a shrine for me to which no one has access; I also know that of all people, you love me the most, and understand me the best. I assure you that no one here would dare, or even want, to say anything bad about you. I'll be so happy and proud when we are together and can bring our work on relative motion to a successful conclusion! When I see other people I can really appreciate how special you are!

The evening before last, Michele's director,[9] with whom we are well acquainted, came over to play some music. He told us how completely useless and almost unbalanced Michele is, despite his extraordinarily vast knowledge. Most captivating is the following little tale, the truth of which can be vouched for by the fact that the person who imparted it to me knows I am friends with Michele and has to take into account that it might get back to him. . . . Once again, Michele had nothing to do. His manager sends him to the Casale power station[10] to inspect and test the newly installed lines. Our hero decides to leave in the evening, to save valuable time of course, but he unfortunately misses the train. The next day he remembers his assignment too late. On the third day he gets to the train station on time, but to his horror realizes that he has forgotten what he is supposed to do. He immediately writes a card to the office saying that instructions should be wired!! I don't think this fellow is normal.

On the question of specific heat, which at the same time concerns the relationship between temperature and radiation process, I've now come up with some very simple conclusions which could perhaps be checked using the experiments that have already been performed. Let the amplitude of a wave train progressing with a certain wavelength in the direction of $+x$ be $Ie^{-\alpha x}$, where I is a constant. Further, let N be the number of radiation resonators (atoms) present in a unit volume. Then α/N shall be independent of the nature of the substance and linearly dependent on the temperature. α/N would then be a function independent of the nature of the metal and of the form $L_1(\lambda) \cdot T + L_2(\lambda)$.[11]

One would first have to find out whether α can be determined by experiments on reflected light, and to what extent the experiments already performed can be used for resolving the question. I'm burning with desire to work my way into this, because I'm hoping it will be possible to make a prodigious step forward in exploring the nature of latent heat. Don't forget to check on the extent to which glass conforms to the Dulong-Petit law.

Hold on to my umbrella for the time being. We'll figure out something to do with it later. If only I could get a position so we can go on our little trip in the summer. Let's hope for the best.

Warmest wishes and kisses, my dear little dumpling, from your   Albert

How's it going with your new apartment *in spe*?[12]

26 *Einstein to Marić*

🐦

Dear Dollie,

It's been such a long time since I received your dear, sweet little letter, and yet I still haven't been able to answer it; I've been so occupied lately, mostly with stupid things. I secretly look forward to leaving home again because it's so difficult to work undisturbed here.

I've begun to have reservations of a fundamental nature about Max Planck's studies on radiation, so much so that I'm reading his paper with mixed feelings.[2] On the other side of the coin, I've gotten a hold of a study on electron theory by Paul Drude with which I am in heartfelt agreement, although it's very sloppy about some things.[3] There's no doubt that Drude is a brilliant man. He also assumes that it is primarily negative electric nuclei without ponderable mass that determine thermal and electrical phenomena in metals.[4] The same idea occurred to me just before I left Zurich.[5]

Michele arrived from Trieste with his wife and child yesterday. He's a terrible weakling, and hasn't a spark of healthy common sense. He's unable to pull himself together enough to do anything in his life or in his studies, but he has an extraordinarily keen mind, the disorderly workings of which I observe with great enjoyment. Last night we talked shop eagerly for almost four hours. We discussed the fundamental separation of luminiferous ether and matter, the definition of absolute rest, molecular forces, surface phenomena, dissociation. He's interested in our research, though he often misses the big picture by worrying about petty things. This pettiness is a natural part of his character, and constantly torments him with all sorts of nervous ideas. The day before yesterday he went on my behalf to see his uncle, Prof. Jung—one of the most influential professors in Italy—to give him our paper.[6] I met the man once before, and must admit that he struck me as being a very inconsequential person. He promised to write to the most important Italian physics professors, Righi and Battelli,[7] on my behalf, i.e., to ask if they need *Assistenten*. This is already a very big step, as he seems to be on quite friendly terms with them. In addition to that, I applied at the Stuttgart Polytechnic, where a position is open,[8] and I wrote to Ostwald again.[9] I will have soon graced all the physicists from the North Sea to the southern tip of Italy with my offer!

You're completely right to have gone to the Engelbrechts again, darling.[10] Judging from past experience, it's still the best place to be. If I've made any money by the time summer rolls around, we'll definitely take our little trip to Venice or someplace. It would make me so happy! I'm really quite a stranger here, and now I see clearly that there's no comparison between the love of one's sweetheart and the love of one's parents. They are as different as night and day. I kiss you then with all my heart and want you to know that your devotion makes me so happy that without it my life would be dismal beyond words. You're right to go to concerts, especially when it's the splendid mass by Bach. Let me know how you liked it.

I have to go to the library now or it will be too late. Hugs and kisses from your   Johnnie

27   *Einstein to Marić*

Milan, Wednesday [10 April 1901][1]

Dear kitten,

If you really knew what kind of hold you have on me, you little witch, you wouldn't be so afraid all the time that I'm keeping things from you, because that really isn't my intention. I also want to tell you right now, darling, that my courage and good mood remain unbroken, especially since I see from your letter that you are cheerful all the time. So today I'm going to give you a detailed report of what I'm up to, because I see that you enjoy it.

During the past week I studied electrochemistry and chemical reactions from Michele's "Ostwald,"[2] and I read about the electron theory of metals in the library. I can easily explain why I'm unhappy about Planck's ideas on the nature of radiation. Planck assumes that a very specific kind of resonator (fixed period and damping) causes the conversion of the radiation energy, an assumption that I have difficulty accepting.[3] Perhaps his most recent theory is more general.[4] I intend to have a go at it now. Drude's electron theory is a kinetic theory of electrical and thermal phenomena in metals, completely in keeping with the kinetic theory of gases. If only we could do without that stupid magnetism which we don't know what to do with![5] I still think that Drude is on the right track, and his idea really does receive quite remarkable confirmation through experiment. I'll tell you more about it another time. I've retreated again somewhat from my idea on the nature of latent heat in solids because my views on the nature of radiation have again sunk into the sea of obscurity. Maybe the future will bring something more sound!

Ostwald hasn't written me (at all), and neither has the professor in Stuttgart to whom I'd turned, and my prospects in Italy are just as bad. But I'm not discouraged in the least, and have already set aside my anger, which was rooted in injured pride for the most part. Battelli is in Pisa and Righi in Bologna. Prof. Jung, Michele's uncle, promised to recommend me there. Since then, I haven't heard anything. But as I said before, I'm not upset about this, otherwise I would have certainly poured out my heart to you, as I've so long been accustomed to doing, my dear, good soul.

Now I'll tell you why I have so much to do. I've been playing the role of tour guide the whole time. Professor Winteler is here for Easter vacation, and I must naturally devote a good deal of my time to him. He's an old village schoolmaster regardless of what he says, but intelligent all the same, and above all, unprejudiced. He ignores the *casus belli*, saying instead, "Girl matters . . . private matters," and prefers to discuss other things with me. I've also been showing around a couple of ladies who are visiting Frau Ansbacher.[6] "Albert has time . . . and he's also a good fellow," they quite rightly say.

Maja is back home as well and has been very nasty toward me.[7] It's hard to imagine that girlish unselfishness is so foreign to her! In contrast, you are so good, my dear, faithful girl! So we'll make our little summer trip *for sure*, even if we have to steal the money to pay for it. Just hold on to that money I gave you—you are the best guardian of it, and no one even needs to know that you have received it from me.

I'm glad that you enjoy living with Frau Engelbrecht again. She is one of the few people who deserve to be called human, and is a very capable person.

Now it's your turn again, darling! I send you my hugs, kisses, and love to reward your faithfulness, which I think of constantly during the day: "Now the dear kitten is hard at work again," but in the evenings I think, "Now she's thinking about me lovingly, and in bed kisses her pillow." You see, I too know how to do it.

Warmest wishes from your　　　　　　　　　　　　Albert

28　*Einstein to Marić*

🐚

Milan, Monday [15 April 1901][1]

My dear Dollie,

Don't be angry with me for not heeding your call to come to Lugano. I was feeling depressed toward the end of last week because once again my job hunting wasn't making any progress. But just wait, love, in a few weeks we'll see each other anyway—surprised, eh? Yesterday I got a letter from Prof. Rebstein at the Technical High School in Winterthur asking me if I would like to substi-

44

tute for him from May 15th to July 15th, because he has to do his military service.[2] You can imagine how happily I would! Granted, I have to teach about thirty hours per week, and this even includes descriptive geometry, but the valiant Swabian is not afraid. And there's more. The evening before last I got a letter from Marcel in which he informed me that I'll probably be getting a permanent position at the Swiss Patent Office in Bern![3] Isn't this too much to ask for all at once? Just think what a wonderful job this would be for me! I'd be overjoyed if something came of it. Just think how nice it is of the Grossmanns once again to have taken the trouble of helping me.[4] This Rebstein is probably Herzog's former *Assistent*, whom we knew.[5]

As for science, I came up with a wonderful idea that allows one to apply our theory of molecular forces to gases as well.[6] You will remember, of course, that the force appears explicitly in the integrals that have to be calculated for determining diffusion, thermal conductivity and viscosity.[7] With gas molecules then, our constants c_α[8] *alone* are necessary for the calculation of these coefficients for ideal gases, and one need not venture into the theoretically uncertain area of deviations from the ideal gas state.[9] I can hardly wait to see the outcome of this test. If it leads to something, we will know nearly as much about molecular forces as about gravitational forces, and only the law of the radius will still remain unknown.[10] Unfortunately, I must also admit that the idea for investigating salt solutions rested on such a weak basis that I think one should first restrict oneself to investigating infinitely dilute solutions in which an interaction between the molecules of the dissolved substance does not yet occur.[11] In such a way one can determine a large quantity of c_α, which could be used for an approximate verification of the hypothesis of the kinship with gravitation. It's perhaps more likely that information about the force law itself may be provided by the

quantities $\dfrac{\gamma - T\frac{d\gamma}{dt}}{\text{volume energy}}$[12] and those integrals from the theory of gases. You couldn't send me Kirchhoff's book on heat, could you?[13] I'd be happy to send the *Popular Books on Natural Science*[14] to your sister, but I'll send them directly from here if that's all right with you. To which address should they be sent?

And how are you, dear little girl? You shouldn't spend the savings on charity, we may need all of it this summer on the Simplon.[15] I'm so happy! Now there's no doubt that we'll be able to go. You have to hand it to that Chinese fellow. I too admire him greatly. So you're my little frog now! We'll see what happens with that. Professor Winteler is leaving today, the Bessos are moving to Trieste tomorrow—I didn't misjudge his erudition, but I completely overestimated his other qualities. He's a frail creature without bone and marrow.

Tender kisses from your   Albert

Best wishes to Fräulein Engelbrecht!

29 *Einstein to Marić*

Zurich [Milan], Tuesday [30 April 1901][1]

My dearest little child,

I just don't let up! You absolutely must come to see me in Como,[2] you sweet little witch. It will cost very little of your time and will be a heavenly joy for me. We'll be back in three days and can still arrange to include Sunday as well. You'll see for yourself how bright and cheerful I've become and how all my frowning has been forgotten. And I love you so much again! It was only out of nervousness that I was so mean to you. You'll hardly recognize me now that I've become so bright and cheerful and am longing so much to see you again, dearest Dollie. Don't fret about the position in Zagreb in case there is interference with your plans.[3] You are a thousand times more important to me than you could ever be to all the people of Zagreb! Who is blocking things there? Tell me a little about it! If you don't get that position, and I get the job in Bern, I hereby appoint you my dear little scientist. There's no need for you to go to a provincial backwater, dear girl—I can appreciate the value of my "pair of old boots," as you've always said, better than you think. And you needn't be jealous of your girlfriends either, because as long as I have strength and desire, I will happily be yours, and you will be a little shrine to me. And my good fortune will be your good fortune. If you knew what you mean to me, you wouldn't envy any of your girlfriends at all; because with all modesty, I think you have more than all of them combined. In any case, come to me in Como and bring my blue nightshirt so we can wrap ourselves up in it, and don't forget to bring your opera glasses. And in addition to that, bring a happy, light heart, and a clear head. I promise you an outing the likes of which you've never seen, even if it rains cats and dogs. As soon as I get the official word from Winterthur,[4] I'll write you immediately so you can decide the day and the hour I can await you.

I'm presently studying Boltzmann's gas theory again.[5] It is all very good, but not enough emphasis is placed on a comparison with reality. But I think that there is enough empirical material for our investigation in the O. E. Meyer.[6] You can check it the next time you're in the library. But this can wait until I get back to Switzerland. In general, I think this book deserves to be studied more carefully.

I was recently struck with the idea that when light is generated, a direct transformation of the energy of motion into light might occur because of the parallel: the kinetic energy of the molecules—absolute temperature—spectrum (spatial radiation energy in the state of equilibrium).[7] Who knows when a tunnel will be dug through these hard mountains! I'm very curious to see whether our conservative molecular forces will hold true for gases as well. If only the mathematically unclear concept of molecular size does not again reveal itself in the formation of the trajectories of molecules closely approaching each other, and if only the molecule could be treated as a center of force.[8] In any case we will get a quite rigorous test of our view.

Tender kisses from your   Johnnie

30 *Marić to Einstein*

[Zurich, 2 May 1901][1]

My dear Johnnie,

I sent my acceptance of your travel offer yesterday and was really looking forward to it, but don't be mad at me if I decide to cancel it today. I received a letter from home today that has made me lose all desire, not only for having fun, but for life itself. Don't let it bother you though, go ahead and take the trip since you've been looking forward to it for so long. Maybe we can do something together later on. I'm going to lock myself up and work hard, because it seems I can have nothing without being punished; on the other hand, I don't need anything, and will become as accustomed to this fact as the gypsy to his horse. It doesn't matter sweetheart. Farewell, be cheerful, and if you find any pretty flowers, bring me a few. —Wishes and kisses from your   Dollie

31 *Marić to Einstein*

🐦

[Zurich, 3 May 1901][1]

My dear Johnnie,

I received your dear little letter[2] today and was surprised to see that you hadn't received my letter of acceptance yet. Was it really lost, or did something else happen to it? But I hope you've received it in the meantime. I also wrote you a little card[3] yesterday while in the worst of moods because of a letter I received. But when I read your letter today I became a bit more cheerful, since I see how much you love me, so I think we'll take that little trip after all. I'll arrive in Como then on Sunday morning at 5:00, because I can't afford to waste an entire day traveling a route I already know (aren't you surprised at what a good little sweetheart you have?). And either you will be at the train station already, which seems unlikely, or I'll expect you to be on the first train from Milan. Then we'll walk around part of the lake on foot, practicing our botany, chatting, and enjoying each other's company. —But darling, I need to know if I'll be taking the same route home so I can buy a round-trip ticket, because it's a shame to waste the money. Why didn't you write to Winterthur once more to ask about the teaching job? Maybe they think it is understood; you've been asked and have agreed, after all; or did they intend to write you once more?

And you have so much love for your Dollie, and you long for her so! She's always so happy with your little letters full of passionate love, showing her that you are once again her dear sweetheart, and my God! what sweet little kisses she's saved for you!

I can't wait until Sunday! There are only two days left now, so don't oversleep. Awaiting you with a thousand pleasures, your tormented   Dollie

32 *Einstein to Marić*

ฏ

Dear kitten,

My first greetings from here shall belong to you, darling. First, let me tell you what has happened since our parting. I first went to the Hotel Limmathof, where they decided that there was no room for me after inspecting me from head to toe in my dubious outfit. Then I went to the Hotel Central, where I managed by the skin of my teeth to get shelter for an advance payment of 2.50 francs.[2] This morning Frau Hägi received me very amiably, helped me pack my suitcase, and did everything she could to get me to eat something. She's turned out to be better than we'd thought. Old man Stern was very happy about my call to Winterthur, and Mayer's son,[3] who studied mining engineering, is in a place in eastern Siberia where the ground remains frozen all year long up to a certain depth, and in the winter the temperatures sometimes get as low as 50° below zero. Then I ate lunch at the Orsini with one of the boys from the Bahnhofstrasse, and at 3:00 made for Winterthur. In front of the train station I ran into Rebstein, who scheduled a meeting for me for 10:00 tomorrow morning at the technical school so I can have a chance to see how I'll have to teach. I'm looking forward to my job very much. Rebstein told me that he'd thought of me himself and that Amberg[4] and Ehrat had recommended me to him; it seems there are well-meaning people after all. Then I went to see young Wohlwend at his office;[5] he was enormously happy to see me. I've now rented a room at his landlady's[6] house (Äussere Schaffhauserstr. 38) and will eat in his boarding house. You wouldn't believe how charming and clean my room is! It's a large room with double windows, a porch with a glass door and a lovely view, parquet floor, an unbelievably comfortable sofa, beautiful carpets, a couple of charming pictures—in short, a truly ideal room. In addition to that, everything is sparkling clean. If only you could see it. The house itself is a pretty villa just outside of town, which at this most beautiful time of year looks like a flower garden.

Have you given your dear little feet a good rest, and are you fresh in body and spirit again? If only I could give you some of my happiness so you could never be sad and pensive again. I don't know yet if I'll come on Sunday or not, as it's the only day I can catch Grossmann at home. Maybe I can come early in the morning, have lunch with you, and then go to Thalwil in the afternoon.[7] I'll have to think about it some more.

I have to go pick up Wohlwend now. Best wishes and kisses from your   Albert

33   *Einstein to Marić*

ॐ

[Winterthur, second half of May? 1901][1]
Dear Dollie,

You must be wondering about this strange piece of paper on which I'm writing to you.[2] But I don't think my Dollie will mind, since I don't have anything else to write on. Don't be mad at me for not writing for so long, but I haven't had much to say that you don't already know. In that case I resort to those things that remain pretty and pleasant. I love you, my dear girl, and look forward to seeing you again on Sunday. We can spend another delightful and pleasant day together. The thought of you is the only thing that truly gives my life meaning here. If only thoughts could have a little life and flesh and blood! How beautiful it was the last time you let me press your dear little person against me in that most natural way—let me kiss you passionately for it, my dear, sweet spirit!

So how is your work going, sweetheart? Everything going well in your life? Is old Weber behaving decently, or does he again have "critical comments."[3] The local Prof. Weber is very nice to me and is interested in my work.[4] I gave him our paper.[5] If only we were fortunate enough to pursue this beautiful path together soon, but fate seems to have something against us. This will make things all the better later on when the obstacles and worries have been overcome.

It looks like my parents are broke again, because they asked me to send Maja 50 francs. Their silver wedding anniversary is on August 8th. I'll be so sad during this little celebration! Papa again reminded Michele that he should write me, but so far in vain!

But these things don't matter. I have you and your love after all!

A thousand kisses and an extra sweet one from your

Albert

34 *Marić to Einstein*

[Zurich, second half of May? 1901][1]

Dearest sweetheart,

I just received your second letter and am very happy, immeasurably happy. You're so sweet—oh, how I will kiss you—I can't wait until you come at the end of the week. I think I'll pray to St. Peter to whisper a happy thought to Herr Besso. If you come on Saturday you might be able to sleep here, because one of the boarders is leaving on Friday. I'll ask Fräulein Engelbrecht and I'm sure she will do this for me, if she can. Until then I'll work very hard so that I'm free to enjoy our time together—my God, how beautiful the world will look when I'm your little wife, you'll see. There will be no happier woman in the whole world—in which case the man must also be happy.

Farewell, my sweet little treasure, and at the end of the week come in high spirits to your   Little Woman

35 *Einstein to Marić*

𝔰

Winterthur, Thursday [second half of May? 1901][1]

My dear Dollie,

I don't want to go to bed without answering your dear little letter, which I saw lying on the table when I came home from school—a most sweet little letter. Once again, I'm looking forward to seeing my dear Dollie on Sunday. Cheer up and don't worry—you are my best and dearest sweetheart, come what may.

My theory of thermoelectricity doesn't completely satisfy me. I'm not going to publish it for the time being. Perhaps I'll write to Drude privately to point out his mistakes to him.[2] Tonight I sat at the window for two hours thinking about how to determine the law of molecular forces. I hit upon a very good idea. I'll tell you about it on Sunday.

I still haven't received any kind of response from my sister. She is now at that awkward adolescent age. I hope she comes out of it all right. Michele still hasn't written me either. I think I'll turn to his father and ask him if he can find me a position in an insurance firm. This business of starving is annoying. Other than that, your sweetheart is a capital fellow, if also a bit unlucky.

Writing is stupid. On Sunday I'll kiss you in person. Hugs and greetings from your   Albert

Until our happy reunion! Love!

36 *Einstein to Marić*

&

Winterthur, Tuesday [28? May 1901][1]

My dear kitten,

I just read a wonderful paper by Lenard on the generation of cathode rays by ultraviolet light.[2] Under the influence of this beautiful piece I am filled with such happiness and joy that I absolutely must share some of it with you. Be happy and don't fret, darling. I won't leave you and will bring everything to a happy conclusion. You just have to be patient! You'll see that my arms aren't so bad to rest in, even if things are beginning a little awkwardly. How are you, darling? How's the boy?[3] Can you imagine how pleasant it will be when we're able to work again, completely undisturbed, and with no one around to tell us what to do! You will be well compensated for your present worries with much joy, and the days will pass peacefully and without disturbance or interference.

Yesterday I was alone for the entire day because Wohlwend was in Lenzburg.[4] After taking a very pleasant walk in the woods in the morning I studied Wiedemann's *Annalen*. There I found a numerical confirmation for the fundamental principles of the electron theory which a Dutchman had come up with.[5] I was extremely delighted with this and became fully convinced of the validity of the electron theory.

Wohlwend was also at the Wintelers', but naturally said nothing about me, only a little something to my sister, whom I'm going to write soon. Distance seems to have softened her anger toward me. I'll invite her to spend a Sunday here.

How is our little son? And your dissertation? If I'm not mistaken, Weber once did theoretical work on the motion of heat in metal cylinders.[6] On this basis, see if you can't utilize the tables somehow, if only for appearance's sake. I think he's cited in Heine.[7]

Unfortunately, no one here at the school is up to date on modern physics, and I've already tapped everyone in vain. Would I also become so intellectually lazy if things were going well for me? I don't think so, but the danger really seems to be great. Unfortunately, I learned today that there's considerable competition among mathematicians even in Switzerland. In Germany it's said to be much worse. I've already wondered whether old man Besso couldn't find a job for me with an insurance firm.[8] He's the general manager of a company after all. Don't fret now, I'll do everything I can to look out for you, darling.

So cheer up and write a dear little letter soon to your

Johnnie

37 Einstein to Marić

ɞ

[Winterthur] Tuesday [4? June 1901][1]

Dear Dollie,

What do you think is lying on the table in front of me? A long letter to Drude with two objections to his electron theory. He will hardly be able to offer a reasonable refutation, as my objections are very straightforward. I'm terribly curious to see if he replies, and to what effect. I mentioned of course that I'm without a position. But I've already told you what we are dealing with. I received a card from my sister. She's not going to visit me. Just think, the Wintelers complained about me at the Wohlwends', saying that I'd been leading a life of debauchery in Zurich. —It seems nothing surpasses the "eternal feminine." Byland[2] seems not to have behaved very well either. In his case, the words uttered by a good German sergeant about Napoleon during drill truly apply: "He was a very kindhearted man . . . but dumb, dumb, horribly dumb."

How are you, dear little sweetheart? Let me hear from you soon! Do you still remember how awkward I was the last time? But you can bet I didn't write Drude anything about that. How are your studies going,[3] and the child, and your mood? I hope all three are as well as is to be expected. I'm sending you kisses especially, so you'll never be lacking in good cheer. What the present leaves to be desired will be compensated for in the future—and how. If Michele doesn't write me soon I'll write him once more to see if he can intercede on my behalf with his stern father for a position. If you are a little down and out, your good friends tend to leave you out in the cold. Such is life.

I certainly do have your little jacket. I'll bring it with me the next time I come.

Yesterday I played some music with an older lady.[4] I really enjoyed it. If only you could be there too! You could really use some pleasant diversion. This evening I still have to give a private lesson in algebra.

I'm really looking forward to next Sunday. If only we could be together happily and without worries for a change, without being under so much pressure. I don't think you, poor girl, can imagine such a thing any more than I can. Tender kisses from your

Albert

38 *Einstein to Marić*

[Winterthur] Sunday evening [7? July 1901][1]

My dear Dollie,

I just got home from Lenzburg[2] and found this letter from Drude. It is such manifest proof of the wretchedness of its author that no further comment by me is necessary. From now on I'll no longer turn to such people, and will instead attack them mercilessly in the journals, as they deserve.[3] It's no wonder that little by little one becomes a misanthrope.

But rejoice now in the irrevocable decision I've just made! About our future I've decided the following: I'll look for a position *immediately*, no matter how modest. My scientific goals and personal vanity will not prevent me from accepting the most subordinate role. As soon as I have such a position I'll marry you and have you come to live with me without writing a word of it to anyone until everything's been settled. And then no one can cast a stone upon your dear head, and woe unto him who dares to set himself against you. When your parents and mine are presented with a *fait accompli* they'll just have to reconcile themselves to it as best they can. But as my little wife you can rest your little head peacefully in my lap and won't have any regrets about the love and loyalty you've shown me.

Despite the fact that we're in a difficult situation, I am again quite confident since making this decision. First thing in the morning I'll write old man Besso[4] and go to the director of the local insurance company[5] for additional advice.

Tender kisses, from your   Albert

39 *Marić to Einstein*

[Zurich, ca. 8 July 1901][1]

So sweetheart, you want to look for a position right away and have me come live with you! I was so happy when I read your little letter, and I still am, and always will be happy. And if I don't infect you with my happiness too, sweetheart, then off with my head. But of course, you shouldn't take a really bad position, darling; that would make me feel terrible and I couldn't live with it. Won't our parents be surprised then. By the way, my sister[2] wrote that I should invite you to visit us during the vacation; my parents are probably in a better mood now. Wouldn't you like to come along? It would make me so happy! And just think of the pleasant trip we'd be able to take together! We could get off every so often and go a little ways on foot or make brief stops. At home, everything will be new for you. And when my parents see the two of us together in front of them, all of their doubts will disappear.

Was it pleasant in Lenzburg? There was a terrible storm here Sunday night and I was afraid you might still be en route. I hope you were already indoors, sweetheart. I really wanted to give you some cherries as well, but you wouldn't have been able to take them to Lenzburg. They're waiting for you now, locked up safe and sound. —I've been working very hard and must now devote myself to studying Weber. In the meantime, I spend every moment looking forward to Sunday when I can see you and kiss you again in the flesh, not only in my thoughts, and almost as it pours out of my heart, and everywhere, everywhere.—

What are you up to, sweetheart? Do you have such terrible weather too?

40 *Einstein to Marić*

ॐ

[Mettmenstetten] Monday [22? July 1901][1]

My dear little sweetheart,

Thanks for your dear little card. Nothing came of the position as deputy director. I asked Haller[2] on the phone and was rejected out of hand. I had always expected as much since it's an administrative position.[3]

I'm getting along with my mother a little better now. She suspects something though. She thinks I'll marry you as soon as I have a position. My sister, you see, told her that the postcard was from you.

And now I wish you the best of luck on your exams and hope that they're over soon, dear sweetheart. I think we should take a trip immediately afterwards to put it all behind you, but only over the Klausen,[4] because we have to be careful not to spend too much money, and the price difference is quite significant, don't you think?[5] I'm working on my theory of the surface of liquids all the time, but without any success. All of my efforts since the paper[6] have various shortcomings. That which I recounted to you is completely wrong. I'll prove it to you sometime later.

It's wonderful here in Paradise. From the front veranda one has a panoramic view which continually offers new charms.

Unfortunately there will be all sorts of people visiting us here again (for example, from Genoa),[7] which is something I loathe. If only I could get a position soon and we could vegetate together. This is my innermost wish.

But now my mother is here to drink some coffee.

Tender kisses from your   Albert

Good luck!

41 *Marić to Einstein*

☙

My dearest little sweetheart,

I just received your dear little letter and see that you're not entirely happy either. We're quite a little pair, and yet people here still envy us all the time; this is really too much. Did you really get into an argument with your Mama? You dear sweetheart, the things you must endure for me! And for all this I only have to give you a little bit of ordinary human love. But this isn't so terribly little after all, and if humanly possible, it will make up for quite a bit. And I simply can't believe that your mother won't bury the hatchet with you. She would have to be motivated by ambition and self-love alone, not by love, and such mothers don't exist. You should also remember that your parents have a false impression of me and that it's in my power to place myself in a more favorable light. I think it will take much time and goodwill for reconciliation, but I'm sure it will happen. You know, I've even come up with some techniques to set the thing in motion. For example, if I could ingratiate myself with an acquaintance of theirs whom they look up to a little, then they would already be defeated for the most part (or so I think). I also have a few other ideas on this.

Write to my old man soon, sweetheart, because I'd like to leave on Saturday already, and they should have a letter before I arrive home. Will you send me the letter so I can see what you've written? —I'm traveling with my friend Fräulein Buček.[2] She doesn't know about the mixed feelings with which I make this journey either. Just write a short letter to my Papa; by and by I'll give him the necessary information, the unpleasant news as well.

If you think this is the way Michele will view the affair, then it might be better if you didn't say anything to him. They've all left the plane of pure human feelings behind and are mired in the daily routine of life. You see, though, that in spite of occasional vacillation, your sister has a different attitude toward the affair. I'm really glad that, unlike the others, she hasn't put up a fight against me; quite the contrary.

I'll send the money to Milan right away. Should I send you the other thing too? Or if we see each other once more I'll bring it to you. There's a train that passes Mettmenstetten at 7:56 A.M. on its way to Zug,[3] where it stops for a quarter of an hour and then comes back. Would you like to take this trip with me, darling? Oh, if I could only have you once more to my heart's desire, my dear sweet little darling! If you only knew how much I love you—you are my little everything. So farewell for now, and don't let anything get you down, my darling. Think a bit about your little one, and be hugged and kissed by your   Dollie

Has Prof. Winteler already recommended you in Frauenfeld?[4] Wouldn't it be a good idea for you to introduce yourself to the right people there? That's the custom where I come from; I don't know how it's done here.

42 *Marić to Einstein*

ɗ

[Stein am Rhein, early November 1901][1]

Dear sweetheart,

I'm only writing you a few words because I'm angry that it is my fate to sit alone tomorrow![2] I'm so glad that Kleiner was nice to you![3] And during which vacation do you think you'll be able to do the experiment? If you only knew how happy I am; your last letter made me very depressed.

But sweetheart, don't tell your sister that I'm *here*. I know she won't do anything on purpose, but I'm afraid that something could happen again, as it always has in the past. In all seriousness, don't you think you could do this for me, sweetheart? Promise me. Otherwise, give her my best wishes, and tell her that her dear words that you showed me made me very happy. Just don't give her my address, sweetheart, I'm very worried about it.

Are the flowers still fresh? Did you put them in some water? Don't write your parents anything about me. No more fights;[4] I dread the mere thought of it. The peace right now is pleasant and soothing.

I'm not writing you any more now because I'm angry about tomorrow. So do you agree to keep your mouth shut about where I'm staying, sweetheart? Tell them I'm in Germany.

You sent me such nice books! *The Visit in Detention* is magnificent.[5] It really made me laugh! I also read the one by Forel.[6] I'll write you about it when I'm finished. Have you read the Planck yet?[7] It looks interesting.

But now, great big hugs and kisses from your   Doll

43 *Marić to Einstein*

రో

[Stein am Rhein]
Wednesday [13 November 1901][1]

My dear, naughty little sweetheart,

Now you're not coming tomorrow again! And you don't even say: "I'm coming on Sunday instead." But then you'll surely surprise me, right? You know, if you don't come at all, I may just leave! If you only knew how terribly homesick I am you would surely come.

Are you really out of money? That's nice! The man earns 150 francs, has room and board provided,[2] and at the end of the month doesn't have a cent to his name! What would people say? But don't ever again use that as an excuse for Sunday, please. If you don't get any money by then I'll send you some.

Is your cousin still staying with you? Did he find his ticket? Did he come especially to visit you? One doesn't usually go by way of Schaffhausen, and would normally avoid such a mishap!

There was a fair in Schaffhausen yesterday,[3] but unfortunately I heard about it too late. Otherwise I would have come and bought you something nice, and looked at your tower, possibly spotting my dear little sweetheart in it.[4] If you only knew how much I want to see you again! I think about you all day long, and even more at night, and when you tell me all sorts of sweet things, then I think about you even more.

I'm very curious about what Kleiner will say about the two papers.[5] He should pull himself together and say something sensible. I'd be so happy if you could do the other one soon too.

I'm going to write to Helene.[6] She's surely had her "tiny one" by now.[7] I haven't written her in such a long time because I just wasn't able to bring myself to do it in those awful times. I wrote a long letter once and poured my heart out to her, but then I tore it up. I'm glad I did so. I don't think we should say anything about Lieserl just now; but you should write her a few words every now and then. We must treat her well because she can help us with something important, but mainly because she's so nice and kind and would be so pleased, right, sweetheart? —I read the book by Forel. Stadler[8] said that hypnotism is immoral, and when I read the book I had the same feeling of disgust. Suggestion certainly plays an important role in everything, and I even think that doctors should use it up to a certain point. But such a violation of human consciousness! I feel that Forel distinguishes himself from a quack only inasmuch as he faces his patients with more self-confidence, that is to say "impertinence," based on his more extensive knowledge. But people are such a stupid herd. —I don't understand hypnotic sleep, maybe it can't be understood at all, maybe it doesn't exist at all! I think this is suggestion as well, or at best autosuggestion, because I think most of the experiments he cites are dishonest (sorry!). I'll tell you why later.

But farewell for now, my little one, my darling. Do you think of me too sometimes, but nice, sweet thoughts? So you're coming on Sunday now, right, sweetheart? I've already saved up so many kisses that if the bowl overflows they'll all be gone. So for now, tender kisses and best wishes from your   Dollie

who is very angry with you right now.
I'll tell you a funny story about something that happened to you once.

44   *Einstein to Marić*

𝕤

[Schaffhausen] Thursday [28 November 1901][1]

Dear sweetheart!

It's been three days and as many nights now since I've received a letter from you. It must have gotten lost, because I'm sure you wouldn't make me wait so long otherwise. Did you finally receive the two or three letters I sent to Kać, and the one to Novi Sad?[2] I think your postmen have used them for kindling, or even . . . *horribile dictu*, but I won't say it. Don't worry, from now on I'll say in each letter that I'm going to write you often, so you know that everything is fine, except for the negligent postal service.

Besides the lack of news I am quite well, and almost always in good spirits. If only I were certain that this letter would arrive safely in your hands. Check in Kać, and make sure that those letters aren't actually there! It's hard to believe.

My new room is really quite comfortable, though its only decorations are myself and the old red lampshade, which Frau Baumer said was more trouble than she would have gone to even for her own Karl.[3] But I thought to myself: "If my dear little sweetheart were here, she would do so many different things for me"—as I would for her. I've already written you about these things, but who knows whether you received them or not. I cannot say how happy I am that your parents have calmed down and now trust me more. I also know I deserve it, and their little kitten will be getting a good husband as soon as we can work things out. I've given up on the position in Bern, as no notice has appeared in the newspaper yet.[4]

Write to me in detail about how you spend each day, so I can fantasize about what you're up to; such a thing shouldn't be too difficult to imagine. I haven't been seeing anyone in my free time, and live here as if in total isolation. Nearly every day I take a short walk to get some fresh air, and spend the rest of my free time studying Voigt's theoretical physics,[5] from which I've already learned a great deal. The night before last the local music teachers held an evening of chamber music, which was delightful beyond my expectations.[6] I have no news from Kleiner so far. I'm sure he won't dare reject my dissertation,[7] otherwise the shortsighted man is of little use to me. If I had to be at his beck and call in order to become a professor—I'd rather remain a poor private tutor.

Should I send you a book, sweetheart, or do you have another wish I can fulfill? Don't be afraid to write me about it—and write me often. Each letter brings me great joy. They are the only human pleasures here to warm my soul. They must take the place of wife, parents, friends, and companions, and they do a good job of it. Of course, it would be much nicer if you were here with me, as in our happy days as students in Zurich. As soon as I receive my doctorate, I'll apply for a secure position. Some day fate will smile on us. When you get tired of being at home, come to me. You will always be welcomed with open arms, and somehow we'll manage.

Write soon, and with an open heart. Sweet kisses from your

Albert Johnnie

45 *Einstein to Marić*

Schaffhausen, Thursday [12 December 1901][1]

My dear little sweetheart,

I received the belly-aching letter that you were so sweet to have written me in bed. But I'm not worried at all, because I see from your good mood that the situation isn't so bad after all. Just take good care of yourself and keep your spirits up, and be happy about our dear Lieserl, whom I secretly (so Dollie doesn't notice) prefer to imagine a Hanserl.[2]

I have a lot of news again, some good and some bad. First, it should be pointed out that Kleiner hasn't written me yet. Second, Louis's mother is making a fuss about our "emigration-to-Bern" project.[3] She explained that the money doesn't matter (she must have almost as much as the two of us combined, don't you think?); but it's clear that she shouldn't have to deal with the additional worry and excitement it would cause her, as she already has quite enough of that right now (her husband suddenly became insane in August). So I advised him to give up on the plan. Besides, there was always the danger of falling between two chairs if I'd persisted with the idea. Just think what a horrible mess we'd be in then! Therefore I decided to settle in here as comfortably as possible. I went to Nüesch[4] and told him he should pay me for the meals, so I can perhaps save a little money. Flushed with anger, he said he'd think about it. Then he talked it over with his fair wife.[5] When I came back in the evening he was very rude and said in an authoritative tone: "You know what our conditions are, there is no reason to deviate from them. You should be satisfied with the treatment you're getting." To this I said: "Good, as you wish. I'll have to give in for the time being,—but I will be able to find living conditions that are better suited to me." (Imagine the nerve, in my position!) He understood this and immediately softened. He realized that I'm less concerned with saving money than with not wanting to eat with him and his good family,[6] and swallowing his anger, he asked me in the softest possible voice: "Would you be satisfied if I provided you with your meals elsewhere, in a restaurant perhaps?" I immediately understood why he wanted to do that—so it would be impossible to control how much he steals from the 4,000 francs set aside for me. So I happily agreed, and departed, commenting that he should make the arrangements as soon as possible. I had after all achieved my purpose. Now they're in a vicious rage against me, but now I'm just as free as any other man. I've already eaten there today. It's very cozy, and I've made a couple of friends, two young pharmacists. Long live impudence! It is my guardian angel in this world.

As I entered Nüesch's house for the last supper yesterday, just before the subscription concert in which I played,[7] I found a letter from Marcelius[8] lying on my soup plate. It was a very sweet letter in which he said that the position in Bern will be advertised within the next few weeks and that he's certain I'll get it. In two months' time we could find our lives brilliantly changed for the better, and the struggle would be over. I'm dizzy with joy when I think about it. I'm even happier for you than for myself. Together we'd surely be the happiest people on earth. We'll be students (*horribile dictu*) as long as we live and won't give a damn about the world. But we won't ever forget that we owe everything to dear Marcelius, who never stopped thinking about me. I make a solemn vow always to help gifted young men whenever I can. The only problem that still needs to be resolved is how to keep our Lieserl with us; I wouldn't want to have to give her up. Ask your Papa;[9] he's an experienced man, and knows the world better than your overworked, impractical Johnnie. She shouldn't be stuffed with cow milk, because it might make her stupid. (Yours would be more nourishing, right?)

I've had another obvious, but important scientific idea about molecular forces. You know that no noticeable generation of heat takes place when two neutral liquids are mixed together.[10] From this it follows, according to our theory of molecular forces, that there must be an approximate proportionality between our constants Σc_α[11] and the molecular volumes of the liquids.[12] If this were true, then the molecular-kinetic theory of liquids would be done for.[13] I want to see if I can scare up Ostwald or Landolt during the vacation.[14] I'll either stay here (to save money) or go to Zurich and work (this is more important than any secondary considerations).

My student just told me that the Bern project isn't so impossible after all. His mother seems to have come around a bit. This isn't very important to me anymore, though it would still be great fun.

Be happy, my dear, faithful little sweetheart. Give your parents my warmest wishes, as I hold you close to my heart. Your

Johnnie

46 *Einstein to Marić*

ॐ

Schaffhausen, Tuesday [17 December 1901][1]

My dear sweetheart,

It's really a comical life I'm leading here, entirely in the sense of Schopenhauer's solitude.[2] Except for my student I don't talk to anyone all day. Even Herr Baumer's[3] company is boring and uninteresting to me. I always find that my best company is when I'm alone, except when I'm with you. And I miss you so much. I think every regular fellow should have a girl.

I want so much to be with you, even if you do have a "funny figure" as you've already written twice. Make me a drawing of it, a really pretty one! I'd be so happy if you made me a pillow. But then you'll also have to make the stuffing for it (for the pillow's sake), because I have no idea where mine are. You know what a dreadful mess my worldly possessions are in—it's lucky I don't have much. I like my new eating arrangement at the inn.[4] In any case, it's quite an improvement so it doesn't seem so desirable to move to Bern with my student after all. But the people I eat with seem stupid and common. So I sit eating like a nutcracker and play with my knife and fork between courses while looking out the window. These people must think I've never laughed in my life; but then, they've never seen me with my Dollie.

I'm busily at work on an electrodynamics of moving bodies, which promises to be quite a capital piece of work. I wrote to you that I doubted the correctness of the ideas about relative motion, but my reservations were based on a simple calculational error. Now I believe in them more than ever. I'm going to stop by the interminably slow Kleiner's place on Thursday since he still hasn't responded. I want to convince him to let me work during Christmas vacation. I wonder if I'll succeed. It's really terrible, all the things these old philistines put in the path of people who aren't of their ilk. They instinctively view every intelligent youth as a danger to their fragile dignity, or so it seems to me. But if he dares to reject my dissertation, then I'll publish his rejection along with my paper and make a fool of him. But if he accepts it, then we'll see what good old Herr Drude has to say[5]. . . . A fine bunch, all of them. If Diogenes were alive today, he'd be looking in vain for an *honest* person with his lantern.

Soon I'll mail a little package for you and your sister—nothing to eat, but much to read. Don't get your hopes up because it's not much, but it comes from the heart. You must be content with it and think: "If my sweetheart had more, he'd send it to me." So think along these lines, all right?

Give your mother my best wishes, and tell her I'm looking forward to the spanking with which she will do me honor some day.

But for you, warm hugs and kisses from your　　Johnnie

I'll send you the money as soon as you want it. It seems strange for it to be coming from me. What do you think?

47　*Einstein to Marić*

Schaffhausen, Thursday [19 December 1901][1]

My dear sweetheart,

Good news once again! But wait, first a belated congratulations on your birthday yesterday, which I'd forgotten once again. But listen up, and let me hug you and kiss you with glee! Haller has personally written me a friendly letter asking me to apply at once for a newly created position in the Patent Office! There's no doubt anymore. Grossmann has already congratulated me. I'll dedicate my dissertation to him to show my appreciation somehow.[2] He's shown me that he's a good fellow! And soon you'll be my happy little wife, just watch. Now our troubles are over. Only now that this terrible weight is off my shoulders do I realize how much I love you. I'm certain that everything will work out for us soon. Soon I'll be able to take my Dollie in my arms and call her my own in front of the whole world. Soon you'll be my "student" again, like in Zurich. Looking forward to it?

I spent all afternoon at Kleiner's in Zurich telling him my ideas about the electrodynamics of moving bodies, and we talked about all sorts of other physics problems. He's not quite as stupid as I'd thought, and moreover, he's a good fellow. He said I can count on him for a recommendation anytime. Isn't that nice of him? He has to be away during the vacation and hasn't read my paper yet.[3] I told him to take his time, and that it's not pressing. He advised me to publish my ideas on the electromagnetic theory of light of moving bodies along with the experimental method.[4] He found the method I've proposed to be the simplest and most expedient one imaginable. I was quite happy about the success. I'll write the paper in the next few weeks for sure. I'll stay here during the vacation, but spend Christmas Eve and Christmas with my sister in the cozy winter solitude of Paradise. If only you could be there too! But our own paradise will come soon enough. I'm absolutely crazy with happiness. It isn't certain whether the Englishman will come with me to Bern yet or not—but under the circumstances, I don't really care. That wretched old fellow will be stunned when I tell him! He's such a dreadful scoundrel. I've heard some really hair-raising things about him.

Hugs and kisses from your   Johnnie

The package of books is already on its way.

48 *Einstein to Marić*

[Schaffhausen] Saturday
[28 December 1901][1]

My dearest little sweetheart,

I'm writing to you again already because I can't bear not to write you. I have such a precious little sweetheart, and my what a nice little package she's sent me! She even hid a nice bit of tobacco in it as well as a dear, dear letter. I've been reveling in them all day long. The goodies are unbelievably delicious, and for each one I eat I give you a kiss in my thoughts. I've already eaten almost half of them even though they came only yesterday at noon. I'm not in a bad mood at all. I'm beside myself at the thought of the opportunities that beckon to us in the near future. Have I told you yet how rich we'll be in Bern? According to the advertisement the minimum salary is 3,500 francs, and can climb to 4,500 francs. Ehrat doesn't think you can get by on 4,000 with a wife. We'll just have to prove how splendidly this can be done, right sweetheart! Besides, in Zurich we got by on barely half of that and had a good time anyway. It's amusing how impractical people can be. It is supposed to be more expensive in Bern than in Zurich, but this too shouldn't be much of a problem.

Michele gave me a book on the theory of ether written in 1885.[2] Its views are so outdated, you would think it came from antiquity. It makes you realize how quickly knowledge advances these days. I want to get down to business now and read what Lorentz and Drude have written about the electrodynamics of moving bodies.[3] Ehrat will have to get the literature for me.[4] Grossmann is doing his dissertation on a subject that is related to fiddling[5] and non-Euclidean geometry.[6] I don't know exactly what it is. Ehrat wants to do his dissertation with Geiser,[7] because he's afraid to do it on that silly topic that Minkowski proposed. See, your Johnnie finished his paper first,[8] despite being hounded in the process. When you're my dear little wife we'll diligently work on science together so we don't become old philistines, right? My sister seemed so crass to me. You'd better not get that way—it would be terrible. You must always be my witch and street urchin. I want to see you so badly. If I could only have you for a little while! Everyone but you seems foreign to me, as if they were separated from me by an invisible wall. You should hear Ehrat talking about marriage. It's so funny. He speaks of it as if it were a bitter medicine that has to be taken dutifully. His wife will find this attitude amusing! Just think of how differently people view something that is one and the same. It's very funny.

Tender kisses from your   Johnnie

49 *Einstein to Marić*

Bern, Tuesday [4 February 1902][1]

My dearest sweetheart,

Poor, dear sweetheart; what you've had to suffer if you can't even write me yourself anymore! It's such a shame that our dear Lieserl must be introduced to the world this way![2] I hope you are bright and cheerful by the time my letter arrives. I was frightened out of my wits when your father's letter came because I had already sensed something wrong. All other fates are nothing compared to this. My first reaction was to remain a teacher at old Nüesch's for two more years[3] if that could bring you health and happiness; but now you see that it really is a Lieserl, just as you'd wished. Is she healthy, and does she cry properly? What are her eyes like? Which one of us does she more resemble? Who is giving her milk? Is she hungry? She must be completely bald. I love her so much and don't even know her yet! Couldn't you have a photograph made of her when you've regained your health? Is she looking at things yet?

Now you can make observations. I'd like to make a Lieserl myself sometime—it must be fascinating! She's certainly able to cry already, but won't know how to laugh until much later. Therein lies a profound truth. When you feel a little better you'll have to draw a picture of her!

It's wonderful here in Bern. An ancient, thoroughly pleasant city in which one can live exactly as in Zurich. There are very old arcades stretching along both sides of the streets, so you can walk from one end of the city to the other in the worst rain without getting noticeably wet. The houses are exceptionally clean on the inside; I saw this everywhere yesterday when I was looking for a room. It's done me a world of good to have escaped from those unpleasant surroundings. I've already taken care of placing an advertisement in the local newspaper.[4] I hope something comes of it. If I only had two lessons a day, I could save a little for you. I have a large, pleasant room with a very comfortable sofa. It only costs 23 francs. That's not too much. I also have six upholstered chairs and three cabinets; you could hold a meeting in this place. Here's the floor plan:

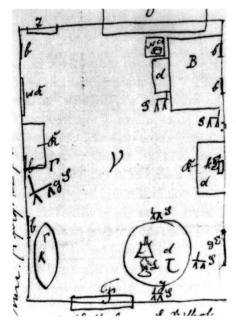

B – little bed
b – little picture
d – little table cloth
gS – giant armchair
gΣ – giant mirror
J – Johnnie
K – chest of drawers
κ – sofa
kΣ – small mirror
N – chamberpot and table
F – little window
O – oven
S – little chair
T – doors
τ – table
v – nothing
U – little clock
Γ – will you look at that!

But now I ask you as nicely as I can to get better soon! Best wishes to your mother too. But for you, tender kisses from your loving   Johnnie

Gerechtigkeitsgasse 32

Bern

(c/o Frau Sievers)[5]

50 *Einstein to Marić*

🖎

Bern, Saturday [8? February 1902][1]

My dear little sweetheart,

Guess where I was today! At a lecture on forensic pathology with a demonstration *ad oculos*.[2] Friend Frösch,[3] who happens to be here, took me along. I was so fascinated by it that from now on I'm going to go every Saturday. They questioned a sixty-year old woman who attempted arson while senselessly drunk as well as a man accused of fraud who appears to suffer from megalomania (there are some quite interesting cases of pathological swindlers in Forel). Because of his great intelligence, Frösch enjoys the respect of the professor, who turns to him every time he notices something interesting. I then spent the rest of the afternoon with Frösch.

The private lessons aren't going badly at all. I've already found two gentlemen, an engineer and an architect, and I have a few more prospects. I'm going to teach them together, in a kind of private course, and will receive 2 francs per man per lesson. That's not doing badly. The lessons begin the day after tomorrow in the evening.

Right now I'm explaining to Habicht the paper I submitted to Kleiner. He's very enthusiastic about my good ideas and is pestering me to send Boltzmann the part of the paper which relates to his book.[4] I'm going to do it.[5]

I'm almost finished with Mach's book,[6] which interests me greatly, and will finish it tonight.

51   *Einstein to Marić*

[Bern] Monday
[17? February 1902][1]

My little sweetheart,

Putting all of my educational principles to shame, I write you again so soon because I received such a dear little letter from you. Don't be jealous of Habicht and Frösch—what are they to me compared with you! I long for you every day—but I don't show it because it's not "manly"—and I always think: "Joe, you go first, you're the man."[2] But nevertheless, it's true that it's very nice here. But I'd certainly rather be with you in a provincial backwater than without you in Bern. And nothing here makes me happier than receiving a little letter from my sweetheart. Even studying is only half the enjoyment without you. I was recently approached by a man from the Polytechnic in Zurich who is now working at the Patent Office. He finds it very boring there—certain people find everything boring—I'm sure I'll like it and will be grateful to Haller for as long as I live.[3] He also told me that the advertisement in the *Bundesblatt* doesn't even mention "physics," but only polytechnic-mechanical training.[4] Haller put this in for my sake. Furthermore, the selection of civil servants takes place in such a way that Haller makes the proposal, and the Swiss Federal Council makes the appointment; so there's hardly any doubt about it. He also said, a little scornfully, that the position was of the lowest rank, and that hardly anyone is likely to compete with me for it. I was not a little pleased to hear that. We could care less about being "on top!"

52   *Einstein to Marić*

ぷ

Bern, Saturday evening
[28 June 1902 or later][1]

My dear little sweetheart,

I just came merrily from the garden with Ehrat, Solovini,[2] and another young man I know from Schaffhausen[3] who came along to Bern just to visit me. Tomorrow I'm going with them to the Beatenberg[4] near Thun, and on Monday they'll leave, which will make me very happy. I'd rather be going with you up to the Beatenberg than with a group of men—I'm a man myself after all. When I'm not with you, I think about you with such tenderness as you can hardly imagine; this in spite of the fact that I'm a bad boy when I'm with you. But just wait, next Sunday or the Sunday after we'll go on an outing and will leave by Saturday evening already! Then, once again, I'll kiss you and squeeze you to my heart's desire all night long. Ehrat suffers terribly from nervousness, despite his very pleasant life. Just think if he had to do my work![5] I don't think he'd last a fortnight. He really ought to have a little sweetheart like I do, someone who loves him, and who can teach him a little of the poetry of life. Then he would learn that there is such a thing as a passionate, carefree life, and that it is not only filled with worries and frowns.

Farewell my little sweetheart; we'll meet Monday at 6:00 at the little tower.

Kisses from your   Johnnie

53 Einstein-Marić to Einstein

🐦

Dear Johnnie,

I'm already in Budapest. It's going quickly, but badly. I'm not feeling well at all.[1] What are you up to, little Johnnie? Write me soon, okay?

Your poor   Dollie

54 Einstein to Einstein-Marić

🐦

Bern, Friday [19? September 1903][1]

Dear Dollie,

I'm not the least bit angry that poor Dollie is hatching a new chick. In fact, I'm happy about it and had already given some thought to whether I shouldn't see to it that you get a new Lieserl.[2] After all, you shouldn't be denied that which is the right of all women. Don't worry about it, and come back content. Brood on it very carefully so that something good will come of it.

I'm very sorry about what has befallen Lieserl. It's so easy to suffer lasting effects from scarlet fever. If only this will pass. As what is the child registered?[3] We must take precautions that problems don't arise for her later.

Now, come to me again soon. Three and a half weeks have already passed and a good little wife shouldn't leave her husband alone any longer. Things don't yet look nearly as bad at home as you think. You'll be able to clean up in short order.

I now get along with Haller better than ever. He is very friendly, and recently, when a patent agent complained about my evaluation and based his argument on a decision of the German Patent Office, he said I was right on all points. You'll see, I'll get ahead so we don't have to starve. If only my mother could get a position in Berlin, then we'd be good shape.[4] It also seems quite certain that Oberlin, who is well disposed towards me, will become a deputy administrator.[5] Luigi will soon be in Hechingen.[6] I wonder if he'll still come to Bern.

Come soon. Kisses from   Johnnie

Best wishes to all.

Notes

ฮ์

REFERENCES IN THE INTRODUCTION

two Serbian biographers ... Desanka Trbuhović-Gjurić, *Im Schatten Albert Einsteins* (Bern: Paul Haupt, 1983), and Dord Krstić, Appendix A, in *Hans Albert Einstein: Reminiscences of His Life and Our Life Together*, by Elizabeth Roboz Einstein (Iowa City: Iowa Institute of Hydraulic Research, 1991).

the corpse of my childhood ... Einstein to Michele Besso, 6 March 1952 (published in *Einstein/Besso* 1972, p. 464).

be careful that Einstein doesn't talk you to death ... Paul Ehrenfest to Tatiana Ehrenfest, 18 January 1912 (Museum Boerhaave, Leiden, Paul Ehrenfest Archive, EPC: 2, Sec. 5).

the little, insignificant foolish darling ... Einstein to Marie Winteler, 21 April 1896 (*CPAE*, Vol. 1, Doc. 18).

soon make things hot for the man ... Einstein to Jost Winteler, 8 July 1901 (*CPAE*, Vol. 1, Doc. 115).

one of the pioneers of X-ray research in Switzerland ... *Conrad Wüest* ... For evidence of Conrad Wüest's work on X rays, see, e.g., his obituaries in the *Aargauer Tageblatt*, 27 February 1904, and *Programm der städtischen Schulen in Aarau. Schuljahr 1903–1904* (Aarau: Sauerländer, 1904).

he expressed a desire to become a theoretical scientist ... In an essay written for a French exam, 18 September 1898 (*CPAE*, Vol. 1, Doc. 22).

Besso ... who had passed on the fund of applied thermodynamics ... Michele Besso to Aurel Stodola, 22 August 1941 (ETH Bibliothek, Zurich, Hs. 496: 5).

Besso pointed out ... "Brownian Motion" ... Draft letter Michele Besso to Carl Seelig, 15 January 1954 (ETH Bibliothek, Zurich, Hs. 304: 196).

LETTER 1

1. Marić entered the Swiss Federal Polytechnic (ETH throughout this edition), School for Mathematics and Science Teachers, Mathematics Section (Section VI A throughout this edition), in 1896. She withdrew on 5 October 1897 and spent the winter semester of 1897–1898 as an auditor at the University of Heidelberg. This letter has been dated by her arrival in Heidelberg.

2. Johanna Bächtold (1852–1927), in whose house in Zurich Marić roomed before her departure.

3. The Neckar flows through Heidelberg.

4. Miloš Marić (1846–1922). The Marić family lived in Kać, a village 15 km northeast of Novi Sad, Hungary (now Yugoslavia).

5. Friedrich Sänger (1875–?), a student at the ETH, withdrew from Section VI A in October 1897.

6. Philipp Lenard (1862–1947), Extraordinary Professor of Theoretical Physics at Heidelberg.

7. The four-hour lecture course was entitled "Theoretical Physics (Heat Theory, Electrodynamics)."

8. *Landolt and Börnstein 1894*, p. 313, gives a mean velocity of 425 m/sec at 0°C.

LETTER 2

1. Marić reentered Section VI A at the ETH in April 1898.

2. Adolf Hurwitz (1859–1919), Professor of Mathematics at the ETH. For the contents of this and the following courses of Albin Herzog (1852–1909), Heinrich Friedrich Weber (1843–1912), and Wilhelm Fiedler (1832–1912) mentioned by Einstein, see *CPAE*, Vol. 1, Appendix E.

3. About 140 students attended the course on mechanics of Albin Herzog in the winter semester of 1897–1898. The course was required for students in the engineering and in the mechanical engineering sections, and in Section VI A.

4. Presumably the course of Ferdinand Rudio (1858–1929), entitled "Number Theory." See *CPAE*, Vol. 1, Appendix E.

5. Presumably Einstein's physics notes (See *CPAE*, Vol. 1, Doc. 37) and those of classmate Marcel Grossmann (1878–1936) on mathematics, which Einstein found indispensable in preparing for examinations (see *Einstein 1955*, p. 147). Marginal comments in Einstein's hand are in two of Grossmann's notebooks for courses by Hermann Minkowski (1864–1909) ("Theory of Functions" and "Elliptical Functions"; see *CPAE*, Vol. 1, Appendix E).

6. Hurwitz was the head of Section VI A.

7. Upon her return to Zurich in April, Marić registered again at the Pension Bächtold.

LETTER 3

1. Dated on the assumption that the letter was written after Marić's return to Zurich from Heidelberg.

2. Presumably *Drude 1894*.

LETTER 4

1. Dated by the allusion to *Drude 1894*, mentioned in the preceding letter.

2. Presumably *Drude 1894*.

LETTER 5

1. Dated by the reference to Marco Besso's death.

2. Marco Tullio Besso (1880–1898), brother of Einstein's friend Michele Besso (1873–1955), entered the chemistry section of the ETH in October 1898. He committed suicide during the night of 27–28 November.

LETTER 6

1. Dated on the assumption that the letter was written on the first or second Monday after the end of lectures for winter semester 1898–1899 at the ETH.

2. The German reads: "Dem Muster das Muster (natürlich ohne Wert)." Einstein is punning on the word "Muster," which in the first instance means "ideal model, example" (e.g., "a model wife, child," etc.). The phrase "Muster ohne Wert" means "a sample without value" (i.e., a fabric pattern sample).

3. A triple pun on "Muster": "das Brieferl wird auch noch nach berühmten Mustern ins Muster fürs Muster gesteckt."

4. Alfred Stern (1846–1936) was Professor of History at the ETH. It is likely that the Ansbacher family of Milan, close friends of both the Einstein and Stern families, introduced Einstein to the Sterns (see *Kayser 1930*, p. 54). Einstein was a frequent guest in the Stern household (see *CPAE*, Vol. 1, Doc. 66).

5. The Swiss border crossing on the Zurich-Milan railroad line.

6. Pauline Einstein (née Koch) (1858–1920).

LETTER 7

1. Dated by the reference to Einstein's arrival in Mettmenstetten, a resort near Zurich (see *CPAE*, Vol. 1, Doc. 48).

2. The Hotel-Pension Paradise, situated above Mettmenstetten.

3. Maja Einstein (1881–1951).

4. *Helmholtz 1888, 1889.* Einstein presumably read these as reprinted in *Helmholtz 1895* (see the following letter).

5. Marić was preparing for the intermediate examination for the *Diplom*, held in early October.

LETTER 8

1. Dated by the reference to Marić's receipt of Einstein's first letter from Mettmenstetten (Letter 7).

2. Robert Markstaller (1865–1933) was the owner of the Hotel-Pension Paradise.

3. The site of a famous Benedictine abbey in the canton of Schwyz.

4. *Helmholtz 1895* (see note 6).

5. *Hertz 1892.*

6. *Helmholtz 1892*, reprinted in *Helmholtz 1895*, pp. 476–504. In addition to his own papers, Helmholtz cites only *Hertz 1890b* in this paper.

7. Hertz's paper on the electrodynamics of moving bodies (*Hertz 1890b*) is reprinted in *Hertz 1892*, pp. 256–285.

8. In Hertz's formulation, some assumption is needed about the motion of the ether in order to develop an electrodynamics of moving bodies. The explanation of a large class of "actual electrical and magnetic phenomena" does not depend on the particular hypothesis made about the motion of the ether within moving bodies or of the free ether. His theory is based on the simplest assumption (that the ether is fully dragged along by moving bodies), although he was aware that this hypothesis probably would not explain all electrodynamic phenomena (see *Hertz 1892*, pp. 256–258).

9. See *Hertz 1890a*, as reprinted in *Hertz 1892*, pp. 211–212, for Hertz's definition of "electrical force."

10. Einstein used the term "electrical mass" as a synonym for electric charge (see *CPAE*, Vol. 1, Doc. 37, note 138). The expression "electrochemical equivalents" is a reference to Faraday's law of electrolysis. *Helmholtz 1881*, reprinted in *Helmholtz 1895*, pp. 52–87, is an influential account of the significance of Faraday's law, in which Helmholtz drew the conclusion that "atoms of electricity" exist (p. 69). See also *Helmholtz 1893*, as reprinted in *Helmholtz 1895*, pp. 505–525, especially p. 506.

11. This is the divergence of the "electrical force" in Hertz's terminology and notation (see *Hertz 1892*, p. 227). For Hertz, this divergence defined the density of "free electricity" which, in empty space, is equal to the density of "true electricity."

12. The term "magnetisms" was used by Hertz to denote elementary magnets. He did not exclude the possibility that they are produced by electric currents (see ibid., p. 243).

13. Conrad Wüest (1849–1904) was a physicist and rector of the Aarau district school from ca. 1889 until 1904. Einstein planned to do scientific work with him (see *CPAE*, Vol. 1, Doc. 48), probably involving cathode-ray tubes and the radiation experiments mentioned in the previous sentence.

14. Julie Koch (1857–1914).

15. Written on the envelope in the hand of Einstein's mother, Pauline Einstein.

16. Written on the envelope in the hand of Einstein's sister, Maja Einstein.

LETTER 9

1. Dated on the assumption that this letter was written after the preceding letter and before the following one.

2. Letters 7 and 8.

3. The Marić home in Kać.

4. Professor Wilhelm Fiedler administered the intermediate examination in descriptive and projective geometry.

5. Professor Albin Herzog administered the intermediate examination in mechanics.

6. Stephanie Markwalder (1851–1934), Klosbachstrasse 87, was Einstein's landlady from September 1898 until October 1899. The notebook is the first part of Einstein's notes on H. F. Weber's course (see *CPAE*, Vol. 1, Doc. 37).

7. The intermediate examination began on 2 October.

LETTER 10

1. Dated by the reference to library closures.

2. The preceding letter.

3. The Zurich municipal library (now part of the central library) was closed during the week of 11 September.

4. Presumably *Helmholtz 1897* (see the next letter); perhaps *Boltzmann 1896, 1898*, which Einstein finished reading a year later (see Letters 21 and 22). Mach's *Mechanik* (*Mach 1897*) and *Wärmelehre* (*Mach 1896*) were recommended to Einstein by Michele Besso in about 1897. Einstein remembered reading the *Mechanik* first (see Einstein to Michele Besso, 6 January 1948, and Einstein to Carl Seelig, 8 April 1952).

5. The reference to "the velocity of the propagation of light in transparent bodies" suggests that Einstein may have had in mind some variant of Fizeau's experiment (see *Fizeau 1851*).

LETTER 11

1. Dated on the assumption that this letter was written before Marić 's intermediate examination for the *Diplom*.

2. Wilhelm Wien (1864–1928) assumed a position as professor at the University of Giessen on 1 April 1899. Before that he had been *Privatdozent* at the Technical University in Aachen.

3. Presumably a reference to H. F. Weber, Einstein's supervisor in physics at the ETH. While a student, Einstein "wanted to construct an apparatus to accurately measure the earth's movement against the ether," but was unable to do so because "the skepticism of his teachers was too great, the spirit of enterprise too small" (*Kayser 1930*, p. 52).

4. *Wien 1898*. In this paper, Wien discussed theories of both a mobile and an immobile ether, including that presented in *Lorentz 1895*. He also briefly described thirteen of the most important experiments related to detecting the earth's motion through the ether. The Michelson-Morley experiment is among the ten "attempts with negative results."

5. Einstein's sister entered the second class at the Girls' School in Aarau in the fall of 1899. Einstein is referring to the Winteler family, with whom he boarded while in Aarau.

6. Marić lived at Plattenstrasse 50. Einstein registered at the nearby Unionstrasse 4 on 9 November.

7. "Fiddling" is a play on the name of Professor Wilhelm Fiedler, which in German means "fiddler" (Einstein uses the same expression in Letter 48). Marić had expressed particular concern about Fiedler's portion of the intermediate examination for the *Diplom* (see Letter 9). She passed the examination but received her lowest grade from Fiedler in descriptive and projective geometry.

8. Einstein had passed the intermediate examination the previous year (see *CPAE*, Vol. 1, Doc. 42).

9. Georg Neuweiler (1878–1953) was a student in Section VI A. He took the intermediate examination at the same time as Marić.

10. Marie Winteler (1877–1957).

11. The highest point (871 m) in the immediate vicinity of Zurich.

12. The Säntis is a massif in northeastern Switzerland.

13. *Helmholtz 1897.*

LETTER 12

1. Dated by the references in this letter and in the preceding one to Einstein's return to Zurich.

2. Stephanie Markwalder.

3. Marić's residence at the Pension Engelbrecht.

4. *Helmholtz 1897* (see the preceding letter).

5. See, e.g., *Müller-Pouillet 1888–1890*, chap. 7, and *Braun 1893*, pp. 387–410, for contemporary accounts of thermoelectricity.

6. It seems likely that "latent heat" refers to what Einstein called "the latent kinetic energy of heat" in Letter 24; i.e., to the so-called internal kinetic energy of a body (see Einstein's notes on H. F. Weber's lectures [*CPAE*, Vol. 1, Doc. 37], note 34). The phrase "latent heat in metals" suggests that Einstein was not referring to the latent heat of phase change, of volume change, or of pressure change, all concepts used in contemporary literature (see, e.g., *Bryan 1903*, pp. 75, 76).

7. If "latent heat" refers to the kinetic energy of the constituents of a body (see note 6), then contemporary ideas about the presence of free, "substantive" electrical charge carriers in metals (see, e.g., *Riecke 1898*) might have suggested that such charge carriers also contribute to the specific heat of a metal. Earlier, Max Planck (1858–1947) had given a purely thermodynamic argument for a difference in the specific heats of charged and uncharged bodies (see *Planck 1889*, §3).

8. Presumably a reference to the equipment available in Weber's laboratory at the ETH (see Letter 20).

LETTER 13

1. Dated by Marić's use of the familiar, or "Du," form of address, which she and Einstein adopted around 1900.

L ETTER 1 4

1. Dated on the assumption that Einstein wrote this letter after the end of the final examination for the *Diplom* (see *CPAE*, Vol. 1, Doc. 67).

2. Einstein originally wrote "yesterday," then inserted "the day before."

3. Einstein apparently met his aunt, Julie Koch, in Zurich for the trip to Sarnen in the canton of Obwalden. From here they went to the resort village of Melchtal (894 m).

4. Probably the Hôtel-Kurhaus Melchthal, the largest hotel in the village.

5. The final examination for the *Diplom* (see *CPAE*, Vol. 1, Doc. 67).

6. Sara Bär (1862–1925) of Milan.

7. Maja Einstein returned to the Girls' School in Aarau in August.

8. *Kirchhoff 1897* (see the following letter).

L ETTER 1 5

1. Dated by the reference to Marić's arrival home after taking the final examination for the *Diplom* (see *CPAE* Vol. 1, Doc. 67).

2. Marija Marić (1847–1935).

3. "*Oxistent*" is a play on "*Assistent*," with "Ox" having the same meaning in German as in English. Einstein evidently believed he had a good chance of obtaining a position as *Assistent* at the ETH (see note 7).

4. Hermann Einstein (1847–1902).

5. Konrad Brandenberger (1873–1919) was a student in natural sciences at the University of Zurich. He married Anna Ramsauer (1881–1970) in 1901.

6. A peak (3,239 m) on the border between the cantons of Uri and Bern.

7. Jakob Ehrat (1876–1960), in the running for a position at the ETH as Professor Rudio's *Assistent* (see *CPAE*, Vol. 1, Doc. 77, note 1), was also a candidate for a position at the Thurgau Cantonal School in Frauenfeld. Another candidate there was Karl Matter (1874–1957), one of Professor Hurwitz's *Assistenten*. Einstein hoped to secure a position as *Assistent* at the ETH should either of these candidates be successful.

8. *Kirchhoff 1897*, chaps. 5–7.

L ETTER 1 6

1. Dated on the assumption that Marić's first letter to Melchtal was written shortly after she arrived home.

2. See the two preceding letters.

L ETTER 1 7

1. Dated by the reference in the preceding letter to Einstein's return to Zurich and the references in this letter and in Letter 15 to his trip to Italy.

2. The power plants were located in Canneto sull'Oglio and Isola della Scala. Hermann Einstein was granted a second concession to build and operate a power plant earlier in the year, leading to financial stability in the Einstein household (see, e.g., Letter 19).

3. A Benedictine convent is located in Melchtal.

4. See Letter 21.

LETTER 18

1. Dated by the references in this letter and in Letter 15 to Einstein's departure for Italy.

2. Johanna Engelbrecht (1855–1940), at Plattenstrasse 50.

3. Perhaps a reference to learning about the family business (see the preceding letter).

4. A quotation from Ludwig Uhland's poem, "Swabian Tale."

LETTER 19

1. Dated by the reference to Einstein's arrival in Milan.

2. As *Assistent* at the ETH.

LETTER 20

1. Dated by the reference to the end of the month.

2. Michele Besso was living at Viale Venezia 6 at the time.

3. Anna Besso-Winteler (1872–1944) and their son Vero (1898–1971).

4. (1878–1956). A son of the Einstein family's close friends in Milan (see Letter 6).

5. See *Thomson 1851*. As in Einstein's notes on Weber's physics course (*CPAE*, Vol. 1, Doc. 37), L denotes the thermal conductivity, T, the temperature. Marić's *Diplomarbeit*, which she hoped to use as the basis for her doctoral dissertation, was on heat conduction (see Einstein to Carl Seelig, 8 April 1952: "My *Diplomarbeit* and my first wife's were concerned with heat conduction and were of little interest to me . . .").

6. There is evidence in a "Questionnaire for Municipal Citizenship Applicants," which Einstein completed in October 1900 (*CPAE*, Vol. 1, Doc. 82), that Einstein intended to work on a doctoral dissertation using Weber's laboratory.

7. Marić had a goiter at this time; see also Letter 22.

8. Besso, a technical expert for the Society for the Development of Electrical Enterprises in Italy (see *Einstein/Besso 1972*, p. xxiii), may have been asked to investigate this question by his firm. Studies of radiation from sinusoidal currents had applications in wireless telegraphy (see, e.g., *Wien, M. 1901*). Electromagnetic radiation from a dipole is analyzed in *Hertz 1889*, and radiation from a long straight conductor in *Abraham 1898*.

LETTER 21

1. Dated by the reference to the ETH summer holidays which lasted for two months.

2. Julie and Alice (1891–1952) Koch.

3. In a letter to her friend Helene Kaufler of June/July 1900, Marić mentions "a larger work . . . which I've chosen to be the paper for my *Diplom*, and probably also my doctoral dissertation, which Prof. Weber can criticize." An ETH graduate could obtain a doctorate from the University of Zurich without further examination (see *CPAE*, Vol. 1, the editorial note, "Einstein as a Student of Physics and His Notes on H. F. Weber's Course," pp. 60–62). Though Marić had recently failed the final examination at the ETH (see *CPAE*, Vol. 1, Doc. 67), she planned to retake it in 1901.

4. Karl Matter was awarded the teaching position on 3 September 1900.

5. Presumably a reference to *Boltzmann 1896, 1898*. Copies of both volumes, with several minor annotations by Einstein, are in Einstein's library in Jerusalem.

6. See *Boltzmann 1896*, p. 15.

LETTER 22

1. Dated by the references in this letter and in the preceding one to Professor Hurwitz, and by the following letter.

2. Zorka Marić (1883–1938).

3. One of the Borromean Islands, off Stresa, site of a seventeenth-century palace and garden belonging to the Borromeo family.

4. Possibly a reference to Ferdinand Ruess, Einstein's *Ordinarius* in the fourth and sixth classes at the Luitpold-Gymnasium (see *Kayser 1930*, pp. 33–34). Einstein also maintained contact with Joseph Zametzer, a mathematics teacher at the same school (see Zametzer to Einstein, 7 January 1906).

5. Presumably *Boltzmann 1896, 1898* (see the preceding letter, note 6), and *Heine 1878, 1881*. Heine is cited in *Boltzmann 1896*, pp. 170, 171, and mentioned by Einstein in Letter 36.

6. Henriette Hägi (1843–1906) was Einstein's landlady.

7. A reference to Helene Kaufler's forthcoming marriage to Milivoj Savić (1876–1940) on 15 November.

LETTER 23

1. Dated by the reference to the delay in Einstein's departure for Zurich.

2. Giuseppe Besso (1839–1901).

3. Einstein may already have been reading *Ostwald 1891, 1893*, which are referred to in *CPAE*, Vol. 1, Doc. 92, and cited in *Einstein 1901* (*CPAE*, Vol. 2, Doc. 1).

4. See, e.g., the historical remarks in *Ostwald 1893*, book 2, chap. 1, in particular pp. 542–550, for Ostwald's comments on the last thirty years.

5. See, e.g., *Ostwald 1893*, pp. 788ff.

6. Alfred Kleiner (1849–1916), Professor of Experimental Physics at the University of Zurich.

7. *Einstein 1901* (*CPAE*, Vol. 2, Doc. 1) is dated 13 December 1900. After Gustav Wiedemann's (1826–1899) death, Paul Drude (1863–1906) edited the *Annalen der Physik*.

8. Fridolin Winteler (1873–1953), Anna Besso-Winteler's brother, was a graduate of the ETH in chemical engineering. He was *Assistent* in the chemical engineering institute of the Technical College in Darmstadt. He had been an *Assistent* at the ETH.

9. Einstein's new address in Zurich.

LETTER 24

1. Dated by the references to Einstein's arrival in Milan and to the anticipated reply to the letter to Ostwald (*CPAE*, Vol. 1, Doc. 92).

2. Eduard Riecke (1845–1915), director of the Division of Experimental Physics of the Physics Institute, University of Göttingen. A position as *Assistent* to Riecke, with the exclusive duty of carrying out observations on atmospheric electricity, was advertised for the year 1901–1902 (see *Physikalische Zeitschrift* 2, no. 25 [23 March 1901]: 380). Candidates were requested to submit reports on their courses of studies, dissertations, and any other publications.

3. Einstein remained convinced that Weber would not support his candidacy for a position as *Assistent* (see the following letter, and his letter to Marcel Grossmann of 14 April [*CPAE*, Vol. 1, Doc. 100]). Problems that may have arisen in connection with Einstein's doctoral work under Weber's supervision, and Einstein's failure to get a position as Weber's *Assistent*, may have led him to this conviction.

4. Einstein wrote to Wilhelm Ostwald (1835–1932), Professor of Physical Chemistry at the University of Leipzig, on 19 March, asking to be considered for a position as *Assistent* (*CPAE*, Vol. 1, Doc. 92).

5. Einstein's idea may have been suggested by a reading of *Planck 1900a, 1900b* (see Letters 26 and 27). In these papers, Planck treated a homogeneous dielectric as a collection of identical charged resonators. In *Planck 1902*, he gave a theory of optical dispersion based on this model.

6. See, e.g., the table of elements obeying the Dulong-Petit law in the temperature range $0°–100°C$ in *Wüllner 1896*, pp. 615–616; most of the elements listed are opaque. For comparison of the spectra of some of the listed elements, see, e.g., *Kayser and Runge 1892a, 1892b, 1893*, and *Ostwald 1891*, pp. 268–269.

7. Einstein seems to have been contrasting the specific heats of organic and inorganic substances. The tables in *Landolt and Börnstein 1894*, e.g., pp. 324–330 and pp. 333–338, do not support his claim. For a survey of contemporary results on the absorption spectra of organic compounds, see, e.g., *Ostwald 1891*, pp. 465–468.

8. See, e.g., *Wüllner 1896*, p. 616.

9. Band spectra were held to arise from the complex internal structure of molecules (see, e.g., *Ostwald 1891*, p. 262), and hence could be associated with large internal energies. For the extension of the Dulong-Petit law to compounds, called Neumann's law, see, e.g., *Wüllner 1896*, pp. 621–622.

10. See *Winkelmann 1893a* and *Winkelmann 1896*, p. 351, for data that bear out Einstein's conjecture, and a discussion of the relationship between observed and computed values of specific heats for various glasses.

11. Maja Einstein's school year was almost finished.

12. The Axenstrasse runs between Brunnen and Flüelen, parallel to the eastern shore of the Lake of Uri.

13. Rudolf Einstein (1843–1928) had financed Hermann Einstein's purchase of concessions to build and operate electrical power plants in Canneto sull'Oglio and Isola della Scala. Rudolf Einstein remained his chief creditor until Hermann Einstein's death.

14. Perhaps a slip for Wiener. See *CPAE*, Vol. 1, Doc. 90. The reprint is of *Einstein 1901* (see *CPAE*, Vol. 2, Doc. 1).

LETTER 25

1. Dated by the reference in this letter to Besso's planned return to Milan and by the reference in Letter 26 to his return.

2. The position for which Einstein had applied in Göttingen (see the preceding letter, especially note 2) was filled in April 1902.

3. Einstein presumably had little chance of becoming Riecke's *Assistent* since the position advertised required a doctorate (see the preceding letter, note 2). The second position referred to may be the one to which Dr. Johannes Stark (1874–1957) was reappointed in April 1901.

4. Jost Winteler, who taught at the Aargau Cantonal School but was never Einstein's teacher, was later asked to write recommendations for Einstein (see Letter 21 and *CPAE*, Vol. 1, Doc. 115). As regards his former teachers in Munich, Einstein is perhaps referring to Ferdinand Ruess or Joseph Zametzer (see Letter 22, note 4).

5. For a discussion of anti-Semitism in physics departments of German universities, see *Jungnickel and McCormmach 1986*, pp. 286–287.

6. Bernardo Ansbacher (1845–1914). The Ansbachers were close friends of the Einsteins in Milan.

7. There were four professors of chemistry at the Istituto Technico Superiore di Milano: Pietro Corbetta, Luigi Gabba, Guglielmo Koerner, and Angelo Menozzi.

8. Besso's uncle, Giuseppe Jung (1845–1926).

9. Giovanni Barberis, director of the Society for the Development of Electrical Enterprises in Italy.

10. A city southwest of Milan in the Piedmont region.

11. Einstein's assertion that α/N is a universal function of temperature nei-

ther followed from contemporary theories of optical dispersion nor agreed with experimental results on light-absorption by metals (see, e.g., *Drude 1900b*; for a review, see *Wien 1908*). It was generally accepted that optical parameters of metals, such as α, were approximately independent of temperature (see, e.g., *Drude 1904*, p. 951; *Koenigsberger 1901*). Since volume is an approximately linear function of temperature for metals, the linear temperature dependence of α/N follows for a given metal.

12. Marić returned to the Pension Engelbrecht (see the following letter).

LETTER 26

1. Dated by the references to Besso in this letter and in the preceding letter.

2. Presumably a reference to *Planck 1900a* or *Planck 1900b*. See the following letter for the nature of Einstein's objection to Planck's theory.

3. *Drude 1900c, 1900d*. For an indication of Einstein's later objections to Drude's theory, see Letter 35.

4. In *Drude 1900c, 1900d*, "electrical nuclei" or "electrons," as Drude also called them, do not necessarily have a ponderable mass. Drude preferred to ascribe only an electromagnetic "apparent mass" to them in order to explain why a negligible mass is transported by an electrical current. He assumed two types of charge carriers with charges of equal magnitude and opposite signs. On the basis of experimental data, Drude concluded that the electrical conductivity of the negative carriers was by far the greater of the two.

5. Note that in Letter 24 Einstein described a different idea on the relationship between heat and electricity, which occurred to him on the trip from Zurich.

6. *Einstein 1901* (*CPAE*, Vol. 2, Doc. 1).

7. Augusto Righi (1850–1920), Professor of Physics at the University of Bologna; Angelo Battelli (1863–1916), director of the Physics Institute, University of Pisa.

8. Presumably this vacant position was as *Assistent* to Richard Koch (1852–1924), director of the Physics Institute of the Technical College in Stuttgart, for the winter semester of 1901.

9. Einstein wrote to Ostwald again on 3 April 1901 (see *CPAE*, Vol. 1, Doc. 95).

10. Marić registered again at the Pension Engelbrecht on 29 March.

LETTER 27

1. Dated by the reference to Maja Einstein's recent arrival in Milan. Her school holidays started on 6 April.

2. Book 2 of *Ostwald 1893*, "Electrochemistry," includes a discussion of the theory of chemical reactions. This topic is also discussed extensively elsewhere in *Ostwald 1891, 1893*.

3. In *Planck 1900a*, Planck considered virtual variations that transfer energy and entropy between resonators of different frequencies (see pp. 110–112), but he

used resonators of definite frequency and damping constant to mediate energy and entropy exchanges between rays of that frequency (see p. 107). In *Planck 1900b*, he derived an expression for the entropy of a resonator by considering energy exchanges of a set of identical resonators in equilibrium with the radiation field (see §6). In *Planck 1901* he agreed that criticisms of this derivation are correct (see p. 555).

4. Einstein is probably referring to *Planck 1901*, which appeared in the same issue of the *Annalen der Physik* as *Einstein 1901* (*CPAE*, Vol. 2, Doc. 1). Planck considers only one type of resonator in this paper. Earlier he had suggested the possibility of deriving his black body radiation law by considering a set of resonators having different frequencies (see *Planck 1900c*, pp. 239–241).

5. For contemporary discussions of magnetism and electron theory, see, e.g., *Lang 1900* and *Voigt 1902*.

6. Julie Ansbacher (1845–1933), a close friend of Einstein's mother in Milan. Her sister and niece were visiting (see *CPAE*, Vol. 1, Doc. 104).

7. On the same day, his sister wrote to Pauline Winteler: "I can't bear being with Albert for a single minute because I always get the worst of it and am so often a subject of his mockery that there's nothing for me to do but stay out of his way" (Maja Einstein to Pauline Winteler, 10 April 1901).

LETTER 28

1. Dated by the references in this letter and in the preceding one to the receipt of Grossmann's letter.

2. Jakob Rebstein (1868–1951), Professor of Mathematics at the Technical High School in Winterthur, a Zurich cantonal secondary school, was asked by the director of the school to find a substitute for the period 16 May–11 July.

3. See *CPAE*, Vol. 1, Doc. 100, note 2. The father of Einstein's friend Marcel Grossmann had recommended Einstein to an old colleague of his, now serving as director of the Patent Office.

4. See *CPAE*, Vol. 1, Doc. 100.

5. Einstein and Marić took Albin Herzog's mechanics course in the winter semester of 1896–1897. Rebstein was *Assistent* from 1893 until 1898.

6. See *CPAE*, Vol. 1, Doc. 100.

7. See, e.g., *Boltzmann 1896*, sec. 3, and *Kirchhoff 1894*, Lectures 16 and 17.

8. See *Einstein 1901* (*CPAE*, Vol. 2, Doc. 1), p. 515, and *CPAE*, Vol. 1, the editorial note, "Einstein on Molecular Forces."

9. Deviations from the ideal gas law due to the finite size of molecules and to the existence of intermolecular forces are discussed in, e.g., *Boltzmann 1898*, sec. 1, "Grundzüge der Theorie van der Waals'." See sec. I, §6, and sec. 5, §§52–55, for difficulties encountered in calculating deviations due to the finite size of molecules.

10. See *CPAE*, Vol. 1, the editorial note, "Einstein on Molecular Forces." "Law of radius" probably refers to the function $\varphi(r)$.

11. Simplifications that result from assuming salt solutions to be infinitely dilute are discussed in, e.g., *Ostwald 1891*, p. 780. Einstein applied his theory of molecular forces to completely dissociated salt solutions in *Einstein 1902a* (*CPAE*, Vol. 2, Doc. 2). In this paper, only forces between solvent molecules and solute ions are considered.

12. *T* is the temperature and γ the surface tension (the derivative should be with respect to *T*). The numerator, "the total energy necessary to form a unit surface" (*Einstein 1901* [*CPAE*, Vol. 1, Doc. 1], p. 514), is proportional to the potential energy per unit volume ("volume energy") of the fluid; the proportionality factor depends on two constants that depend, in turn, on $\varphi(r)$, which defines the "force law" (see ibid., p. 516).

13. *Kirchhoff 1894*.

14. *Bernstein 1853–1857*. A copy of these books was given to Einstein ca. 1890 by Max Talmey (see *Talmey 1932*, p. 162).

15. The Simplon Pass (2,005 m) connects Brig in the canton of Valais and Iselle in Italy. Construction work on the first Simplon Tunnel, which began in late 1898, attracted a large number of tourists.

LETTER 29

1. Dated by the reference to Einstein's appointment in Winterthur, and by the reference to this letter in Letter 31.

2. The city of Como lies at the southern tip of Lake Como in Italy, near the Swiss frontier town of Chiasso. See Marić's letter to Helene Savić of May 1901 for a description of this trip (*CPAE*, Vol. 1, Doc. 110), which began in Como.

3. Marić was looking for a secondary-school position at this time (see *CPAE*, Vol. 1, Doc. 87).

4. The director of the school requested approval of Einstein's appointment on 24 April. Einstein received word of the decision on 3 May (see *CPAE*, Vol. 1, Doc. 104).

5. *Boltzmann 1896, 1898*.

6. *Meyer 1895, 1899*. *Boltzmann 1896*, pp. 85, 88, cites the first edition, *Meyer 1877*, for data on internal friction and heat conduction.

7. "Spatial radiation energy in the state of equilibrium" is a reference to black body radiation (for the expressions "spatial energy" and "radiation energy" see *Ostwald 1893*, pp. 12, 1006). *Planck 1900b*, pp. 723–724, notes that the temperature determines both the "mean active force of molecules" and the "intensity of radiation."

8. Differences between the trajectories of colliding molecules treated as centers of force and the trajectories of molecules treated as elastic spheres are discussed in *Boltzmann 1896*, pp. 161–162.

LETTER 30

1. Dated by the reference to this letter in the following letter.

LETTER 31

1. Dated by the reference to her forthcoming trip with Einstein.
2. Letter 29.
3. Letter 30.

LETTER 32

1. Dated by the reference to Einstein's arrival in Winterthur.
2. Both hotels are near the central train station in Zurich.
3. Ernst Maier (1873–1916), son of Gustav Maier (1844–1923), was employed by the Amgun Gold Company.
4. Ernst Amberg (1871–1952), *Assistent* to professors Adolf Hurwitz and Carl Friedrich Geiser (1843–1934). Einstein was tutored (took *Repetitorien*) by Amberg in three courses during his first year at the ETH (see *CPAE*, Vol. 1, Appendix E).
5. Hans Wohlwend (1878–1962), a friend from the Aargau Kantonsschule, was employed by Volkart Brothers, a large import-export firm.
6. Maria Wachter (1862–1933).
7. Grossmann lived with his parents at Alte Landstrasse 156 in Thalwil, canton of Zurich.

LETTER 33

1. Dated on the assumption that this letter was written shortly after the beginning of Einstein's Winterthur appointment.
2. The letter is written on the verso of a blank printed billing form.
3. Marić was working on a *Diplomarbeit* and a doctoral dissertation under Weber's supervision (see Letter 21, note 3).
4. Gustav Weber (1858–1913), Professor of Electrotechnology at the Technical High School in Winterthur.
5. *Einstein 1901* (*CPAE*, Vol. 2, Doc. 1).

LETTER 34

1. Dated by the reference to the preceding letter.

LETTER 35

1. Dated by the references to Einstein's letter to Drude in this letter and in Letter 37.
2. For a discussion of possible objections to Drude's theory, see *CPAE*, Vol. 1, the editorial note, "Einstein on Thermal, Electrical, and Radiation Phenomena."

LETTER 36

1. Dated on the assumption that it was written immediately after Whit Monday (see note 4).

2. *Lenard 1900*, in which Lenard studied the photoelectric effect. He obtained evidence for the existence in vacuum of electric "quanta," emitted from a metal electrode when the latter is irradiated with ultraviolet light.

3. Marić was pregnant and gave birth to a daughter, referred to as "Lieserl," ca. January 1902 (see Letter 49).

4. The day was probably Whit Monday, a holiday.

5. Presumably the article referred to is *Reinganum 1900*: Maximilian Reinganum (1876–1914) was not Dutch, but his article is datelined "Leiden, May 1900"; it is the only article on the electron theory of metals in the same issue of *Annalen der Physik* as the one by Lenard. By use of the equipartition theorem, Reinganum derived an expression for the ratio between thermal and electrical conductivity, which was equivalent to that given in *Drude 1900c*, but which could be evaluated more precisely. Reinganum's result was in good agreement with experiment.

6. See *Weber 1881*, pp. 472–474.

7. *Heine 1881* cites *Weber 1881* on p. 307.

8. Besso's father, Giuseppe, was a director of the Assicurazioni Generali in Trieste.

LETTER 37

1. Dated by the references in this letter and in the preceding one to Wohlwend's visit to the Wintelers.

2. Hans Byland (1878–1949) had been a schoolmate of Einstein's in Aarau.

3. In late July, Marić again took the final examination for the *Diplom* at the ETH.

4. Presumably a reference to Marie Barthelts (1865–1945), who sometimes accompanied Einstein and Wohlwend.

LETTER 38

1. Dated by the references to Drude's letter in this letter and in the following one.

2. Presumably from a visit to Hans Wohlwend's family. Einstein often played music with Wohlwend, his mother, and his sister.

3. Einstein's comments on his dissertation in Letter 46 suggest that it may have contained criticisms of Drude's work.

4. Michele Besso's father, Giuseppe. He had long suffered from gout and died of complications on 1 October.

5. Heinrich Langsdorf (1834–1901) was director of the Swiss Accident In-

surance Company. Earlier, he had taught mathematics and physics at the Technical
High School in Winterthur and served as its director.

LETTER 39

1. Dated on the assumption that it is a reply to Letter 38.
2. Zorka Marić.

LETTER 40

1. Dated by the reference to Marić's forthcoming examinations.
2. Friedrich Haller (1844–1936), director of the Swiss Patent Office.
3. Positions at the Patent Office were classified as either administrative or
technical (see *Morf 1963*, p. 147). A position as administrative deputy (*Adjunkt*)
was advertised in the *Schweizerisches Bundesblatt* 53, no. 27 [3 July 1901]: 922,
with applications due by 22 July.
4. A mountain pass (1,949 m) in the canton of Uri.
5. Presumably compared to the cost of a trip to the Simplon (see Letter 28).
6. *Einstein 1901* (*CPAE*, Vol. 2, Doc. 1).
7. Presumably a reference to a visit by members of the Jacob Koch family.

LETTER 41

1. Dated by the reference to Marić's departure for home, after she failed the
final examination for the *Diplom*.
2. Auguste Buček (1873–?), a medical student, was returning to her home in
Croatia. She presumably met Marić at the Pension Bächtold while they both lived
there.
3. The capital of the canton of Zug.
4. There was a vacant "teaching position for mathematical-technical subjects in the industrial division" at the Thurgau Cantonal School in Frauenfeld. Applications were due by 27 July.

LETTER 42

1. Dated by postmarks on the letter paper which read: "Schaffhausen
31.X.01.XII." The letter paper is addressed in Einstein's hand: "Fräulein Mileva
Marić Stein am Rhein Hotel Steinerhof."
2. Einstein had another part-time teaching position in Schaffhausen and was
living there, 20 km west of Stein am Rhein. Marić had come to Stein am Rhein
from her parents' home, but remained there only for a short time.
3. Marić may be referring to Alfred Kleiner's response when Einstein submitted two papers to him (see the following letter).
4. Marić was upset over a letter that Einstein's parents had sent to her

parents (see *CPAE*, Vol. 1, Doc. 125). The conflict that resulted may have led to her decision to visit Einstein.

5. *Eckstein 1875.*

6. August Forel (1848–1931), director of the Burghölzli Clinic in Zurich. The book is presumably *Forel 1891* (see the following letter).

7. Possibly a reference to *Planck 1897.*

LETTER 43

1. Dated by the reference to the Schaffhausen fair.

2. Einstein had initially boarded at the private school where he taught, located at Fulachstrasse 22 in Schaffhausen (see *CPAE*, Vol. 1, Doc. 122).

3. The St. Martin's Day Fair was held on 12 November.

4. The building at Fulachstrasse 6 in Schaffhausen in which Einstein roomed in late 1901 had a tower (see illustration 9).

5. The two papers referred to are presumably the doctoral dissertation that he formally submitted to the University of Zurich on 23 November (see *CPAE*, Vol. 1, Doc. 132), and an early version of *Einstein 1902b* (*CPAE*, Vol. 2, Doc. 3) (see *CPAE*, Vol. 1, Doc. 122, in particular, note 5).

6. See *CPAE*, Vol. 1, Doc. 125.

7. Helene Savić gave birth to a daughter, Julka, on 28 October.

8. Marić attended a course, "Outline of Psychology," given by Prof. August Stadler (1850–1910) in the winter semester of 1896–1897.

LETTER 44

1. Dated by the reference to a chamber music concert.

2. In 1900, Marić's father, Miloš, bought a house in Novi Sad, which became the family's winter home.

3. Einstein was renting a room from Cäcilia (1872–1962) and Carl Baumer (1874–1955) at Fulachstrasse 6.

4. Since April 1901, Einstein had been hoping to obtain a position at the Swiss Patent Office in Bern (see *CPAE*, Vol. 1, Doc. 100). In the case of most civil service positions, a notice had to be placed in the newspaper before someone was hired.

5. *Voigt 1895, 1896.*

6. Hedwig Bendel of the Schaffhausen secondary school and Curt Herold of the local *Imthurneum* played music of Mozart, Brahms, and Beethoven at the concert.

7. This dissertation dealt with the molecular forces in gases (see *CPAE*, Vol. 1, Doc. 125).

LETTER 45

1. Dated by the reference to a subscription concert.

2. "Lieserl" is a diminutive of the name Elisabeth, "Hanserl" a diminutive of the name Hans.

3. The mother of Louis Cahen (1882–?), the pupil that Einstein was tutoring, objected to a plan to have Cahen continue his studies with Einstein in Bern.

4. Jakob Nüesch (1845–1915) taught at a Schaffhausen secondary school and directed his own boarding school, in which he had hired Einstein to teach.

5. Bertha Nüesch (1847–1917).

6. The Nüeschs had four children.

7. The second subscription concert of the season.

8. Marcel Grossmann.

9. Miloš Marić was a retired Hungarian civil servant.

10. For the law of thermoneutrality of salt solutions, see, e.g., *Ostwald 1891*, pp. 179ff, and *Nernst 1898*, pp. 557–561.

11. See *Einstein 1901* (*CPAE*, Vol. 2, Doc. 1) and *CPAE*, Vol. 1, the editorial note, "Einstein on Molecular Forces."

12. The proportionality of c and the specific volume may be derived as follows: If no heat is evolved when two neutral fluids are mixed (see note 10), and no external work is done, then the internal energy of the system composed of the two fluids will be unchanged. If the two fluids were at the same temperature before mixing, the internal kinetic energy ("heat content," see *CPAE*, Vol. 1, Doc. 37, note 34) will remain the same. Hence, the internal potential energy of the system will also be unchanged. Einstein's formula for the internal potential energy per unit volume of a fluid (see *Einstein 1901* [*CPAE*, Vol. 2, Doc. 1], p. 516), when applied to this system before and after mixing, yields the proportionality for the two fluids.

13. Presumably a reference to van der Waals's theory, which was often characterized in these terms (see, e.g., *Nernst 1898*, pp. 214ff). Einstein's molecular force law implies that a, the constant in the correction term to the pressure in van der Waals's theory, a/υ^2 (derived in, e.g., *Boltzmann 1898*, §23), is proportional to the square of Einstein's c. Einstein's conclusion that c is proportional to υ then shows that a/υ^2 is independent of υ.

14. Presumably *Ostwald 1891* and *Landolt and Börnstein 1894*.

LETTER 46

1. Dated by the references in this letter and in Letter 47 to Einstein's visit to Kleiner.

2. Einstein read *Schopenhauer 1851* (see *CPAE*, Vol. 1, Doc. 122), which extols solitude (see chap. 5, sec. B, subsec. 9).

3. Carl Baumer, Einstein's former landlord, taught natural sciences at a Schaffhausen secondary school.

4. This may be a reference to the "Cardinal," an inn at Bahnhofstrasse 102 into which Einstein had moved (see *Schneider 1965*).

5. Einstein may have included objections to Drude's electron theory of metals in his dissertation. See the mention of his objections in Letter 37 and *CPAE*, Vol. 1, Doc. 115.

LETTER 47

1. Dated by the reference to Marić's birthday.

2. Einstein did not receive his doctoral degree at this time (see *CPAE*, Vol. 1, Doc. 132). His later doctoral dissertation, *Einstein 1905a* (*CPAE*, Vol. 2, Doc. 15), is dedicated to Marcel Grossmann.

3. Presumably a reference to the dissertation Einstein officially submitted on 23 November (see *CPAE*, Vol. 1, Doc. 132).

4. Presumably a reference to the experimental method for investigating the motion of matter with respect to the ether that is mentioned in *CPAE*, Vol. 1, Doc. 122.

LETTER 48

1. Dated by the references in this letter and in the preceding one to Einstein's Christmas holiday with his sister.

2. The book is probably *Hoh 1885*.

3. *Lorentz 1895* and *Drude 1900a* deal with the electrodynamics of moving bodies. Einstein later stated that when he wrote *Einstein 1905b* (*CPAE*, Vol. 2, Doc. 14), he knew "only Lorentz's significant paper of 1895, but not Lorentz's later work" (Einstein to Carl Seelig, 19 February 1955).

4. Ehrat was an *Assistent* at the ETH.

5. A pun on the name of Grossmann's dissertation advisor, Fiedler, which is the German word for "fiddler." See also Letter 11.

6. Marcel Grossmann's dissertation, supervised by Wilhelm Fiedler, was entitled "On the Metrical Characteristics of Co-Linear Formations." He was awarded the doctorate by the University of Zurich in 1902.

7. Ehrat's dissertation, supervised by Carl Friedrich Geiser, was accepted by the University of Zurich in 1906.

8. Einstein submitted the dissertation on 23 November.

LETTER 49

1. Dated by the reference to Einstein's advertisement in a Bern newspaper of the following day.

2. Marić gave birth to a daughter ca. January 1902.

3. Einstein left Schaffhausen in the middle of the school year, although he was hired for a full year (see *CPAE*, Vol. 1, Docs. 122 and 133).

4. See *CPAE*, Vol. 1, Doc. 135.

5. Einstein's landlady, Anna Sievers (1860–1912).

LETTER 50

1. Dated by the reference to Einstein's pupils.

2. A course on "Forensic Medicine" was held in the winter semester of

1901–1902 at the University of Bern by Karl Emmert (1813–1903), Professor of Public Health. The *Repetitorium* for this course was held on Saturday.

3. Hans Frösch (1877–1938), a medical student at the University of Bern, was an auditor in this class. He and Einstein had been classmates at the Aargau Cantonal School.

4. *Boltzmann 1896, 1898.* Both works that Einstein submitted to Kleiner presumably utilized material from these books. *Kayser 1930*, p. 69, states that Kleiner rejected Einstein's work on the kinetic theory of gases because it "sharply criticized" Boltzmann.

5. Einstein had already contacted Boltzmann (see *CPAE*, Vol. 1, Doc. 85). According to Einstein's sister, he corresponded with Boltzmann until the latter's death in 1906 (see *Winteler-Einstein 1924*, p. 18).

6. Presumably *Mach 1896* or *Mach 1897* (see Letter 10, note 4).

LETTER 51

1. Dated by the references in this letter and in the preceding one to Habicht and Frösch.

2. A variant of a phrase in "The Seven Swabians," a Grimm brothers folktale.

3. Einstein's job at the Patent Office did not begin until June 1902.

4. One requirement was "thorough college training with a mechanical-technical or specialized physics emphasis."

LETTER 52

1. Dated by the reference to Einstein's appointment and on the assumption that he began work on Monday, 23 June.

2. Maurice (or Moritz) Solovine (1875–1958) was a student at the University of Bern. He began an informal discussion group with Einstein soon after meeting him during Easter vacation 1902 (see *Solovine 1956*, p. vi). The group came to be known as the Olympia Academy.

3. Possibly a reference to Carl Baumer.

4. The Beatenberg lies southeast of Thun and on the northern shore of the Lake of Thun. The town of Thun is in the Bernese Oberland, 25 km southeast of Bern. Einstein undertook a number of trips on foot to Thun in the company of Solovine. They would leave at six in the morning, arrive at midday, have lunch, spend the afternoon on the shores of the Lake of Thun, and return by train in the evening (see *Solovine 1956*, pp. xii–xiii).

5. Einstein was provisionally appointed Technical Expert, third class, at the Swiss Patent Office on 16 June 1902 (see *CPAE*, Vol. 1, Doc. 141).

LETTER 53

1. Probably related to the onset of a pregnancy. See the following letter.

LETTER 54

1. Dated by the reference to Einstein-Marić's absence (see the preceding letter).

2. A son, Hans Albert, was born 14 May 1904.

3. This may refer to the intention of the parents to give the child up for adoption. Half a year earlier Einstein-Marić had inquired about teaching positions for her husband and herself in Belgrade, perhaps with the thought of raising the child themselves (see Mileva Einstein-Marić to Helene Savić, ca. 20 March 1903).

4. Einstein was probably providing financial support to Pauline Einstein in order to enable her to liquidate debts inherited from her late husband's business failures (see Letter 24, note 13).

5. Hermann Oberlin (1857–1928), Technical Expert first class, was appointed Technical Adjunct in the Swiss Patent Office on 2 October 1903.

6. Luigi Ansbacher. He left Hechingen on 19 September (see Pauline Einstein to Paul Winteler, 20 September 1903).

Literature Cited

Abraham 1898 Abraham, Max. "Die electrischen Schwingungen um einen stabförmigen Leiter, behandelt nach der Maxwell'schen Theorie." *Annalen der Physik und Chemie* 66 (1898): 435–472.

Bernstein 1853–1857 Bernstein, Aaron. *Aus dem Reiche der Naturwissenschaft. Für Jedermann aus dem Volke.* 12 vols. Berlin: Besser, 1853–1857. Reissued as *Naturwissenschaftliche Volksbücher.* 20 vols. Berlin: Duncker, 1867–1869.

Boltzmann 1896 Boltzmann, Ludwig. *Vorlesungen über Gastheorie.* Part 1, *Theorie der Gase mit einatomigen Molekülen, deren Dimensionen gegen die mittlere Weglänge verschwinden.* Leipzig: Barth, 1896.

Boltzmann 1898 ———. *Vorlesungen über Gastheorie.* Part 2, *Theorie Van der Waals'; Gase mit zusammengesetzten Molekülen; Gasdissociation; Schlussbemerkungen.* Leipzig: Barth, 1898.

Braun 1893 Braun, F. "Thermoelektricität." In *Winkelmann 1893b*, pp. 387–410.

Bryan 1903 Bryan, G. H. "Allgemeine Grundlegung der Thermodynamik." In *Encyklopädie der mathematischen Wissenschaften. Mit Einschluss ihrer Anwendungen.* Vol. 5, part 1, Arnold Sommerfeld, ed., pp. 71–160. Leipzig: Teubner, 1903–1921.

CPAE 1987, 1989 Collected Papers of Albert Einstein. Vols. 1 and 2. Edited by John Stachel et al. Princeton, N.J.: Princeton University Press, 1987 and 1989.

Drude 1894 Drude, Paul. *Physik des Aethers auf elektromagnetischer Grundlage.* Stuttgart: Enke, 1894.

Drude 1900a ———. *Lehrbuch der Optik.* Leipzig: Hirzel, 1900.

Drude 1900b ———. "Zur Ionentheorie der Metalle." *Physikalische Zeitschrift* 1 (1900): 161–165.

Drude 1900c ———. "Zur Elektronentheorie der Metalle. I. Teil." *Annalen der Physik* 1 (1900): 566–613.

Drude 1900d ———. "Zur Elektronentheorie der Metalle. II. Teil." *Annalen der Physik* 3 (1900): 369–402.

Drude 1904 ———. "Optische Eigenschaften und Elektronentheorie. II. Teil." *Annalen der Physik* 14 (1904): 936–961.

Eckstein 1875. Eckstein, Ernst. *Der Besuch im Carcer. Humoreske.* Leipzig: Hartknoch, 1875.

Einstein 1901 Einstein, Albert. "Folgerungen aus den Capillaritätserscheinungen." *Annalen der Physik* 4 (1901): 513–523.

Einstein 1902a ———. "Ueber die thermodynamische Theorie der Potentialdifferenz zwischen Metallen und vollständig dissociirten Lösungen ihrer Salze und über eine elektrische Methode zur Erforschung der Molecularkräfte." *Annalen der Physik* 8 (1902): 798–814.

Einstein 1902b ———. "Kinetische Theorie des Wärmegleichgewichtes und des zweiten Hauptsatzes der Thermodynamik." *Annalen der Physik* 9 (1902): 417–433.

Einstein 1905a ———. *Eine neue Bestimmung der Moleküldimensionen.* Bern: Wyss, 1905.

Einstein 1905b ———. "Zur Elektrodynamik bewegter Körper." *Annalen der Physik* 17 (1905): 891–921.

Einstein 1955 ———. "Erinnerungen-Souvenirs." *Schweizerische Hochschulzeitung* 28 (Sonderheft) (1955): 145–153. Reprinted as "Autobiographische Skizze," in *Helle Zeit-dunkle Zeit. In Memoriam Albert Einstein.* Carl Seelig, ed., pp. 9–17. Zurich: Europa, 1956.

Einstein/Besso 1972 Einstein, Albert, and Besso, Michele. *Correspondance 1903– 1955.* Pierre Speziali, trans. and ed. Paris: Hermann, 1972.

Fizeau 1851 Fizeau, Hippolyte. "Sur les hypothèses relatives à l'éther lumineux, et sur une expérience qui parait démontrer que le mouvement des corps change la vitesse avec laquelle la lumière se propage dans leur intérieur." *Académie des sciences* (Paris). *Comptes rendus* 33 (1851): 349–355.

Forel 1891 Forel, August. *Der Hypnotismus. Seine psycho-physiologische, medicinische, strafrechtliche Bedeutung und seine Handhabung.* 2d rev. ed. Stuttgart: Enke, 1891.

Heine 1878 Heine, Eduard. *Handbuch der Kugelfunctionen, Theorie und Anwendungen.* Vol. 1, *Theorie der Kugelfunctionen und der verwandten Functionen.* 2d rev. ed. Berlin: Reimer, 1878.

Heine 1881 ———. *Handbuch der Kugelfunctionen, Theorie und Anwendungen.* Vol. 2, *Anwendungen der Kugelfunctionen und der verwandten Functionen.* 2d rev. ed. Berlin: Reimer, 1881.

Helmholtz 1881 Helmholtz, Hermann von. "On the Modern Development of Faraday's Conception of Electricity." *Journal of the Chemical Society* 39 (1881): 277–304. Reprinted in *Helmholtz 1895*, pp. 52–87.

Helmholtz 1888 ———. "Ueber atmosphärische Bewegungen." *Königlich Preußische Akademie der Wissenschaften zu Berlin. Sitzungsberichte* (1888): 647–663. Reprinted in *Helmholtz 1895*, pp. 289–308.

Helmholtz 1889 ———. "Ueber atmosphärische Bewegungen. (Zweite Mitteilung.) Zur Theorie von Wind und Wellen." *Königlich Preußische Akademie der Wissenschaften zu Berlin. Sitzungsberichte* (1889): 761–780. Reprinted in *Helmholtz 1895*, pp. 309–332.

Helmholtz 1892 ———. "Das Prinzip der kleinsten Wirkung in der Elektrodynamik." *Annalen der Physik und Chemie* 47 (1892): 1–26. Reprinted in *Helmholtz 1895*, pp. 476–504.

Helmholtz 1893 ———. "Elektromagnetische Theorie der Farbenzerstreuung." *Annalen der Physik und Chemie* 48 (1893): 389–405, 723–725. Reprinted in *Helmholtz 1895*, pp. 505–525.

Helmholtz 1895 ———. *Wissenschaftliche Abhandlungen.* Vol. 3. Leipzig: Barth, 1895.

Helmholtz 1897 ———. *Vorlesungen über die elektromagnetische Theorie des Lichtes.* Arthur König and Carl Runge, eds. Hamburg and Leipzig: Voss, 1897.

Hertz 1889. Hertz, Heinrich. "Die Kräfte elektrischer Schwingungen, behandelt nach der Maxwell'schen Theorie." *Annalen der Physik und Chemie* 36 (1889): 1–22. Reprinted in *Hertz 1892,* pp. 147–170.

Hertz 1890a ———. "Ueber die Grundgleichungen der Elektrodynamik für ruhende Körper." *Annalen der Physik und Chemie* 40 (1890): 577–624. Reprinted in *Hertz 1892,* pp. 208–255.

Hertz 1890b ———. "Ueber die Grundgleichungen der Elektrodynamik für bewegte Körper." *Annalen der Physik und Chemie* 41 (1890): 369–399. Reprinted in *Hertz 1892,* pp. 256–285.

Hertz 1892 ———. *Untersuchungen über die Ausbreitung der elektrischen Kraft.* Leipzig: Barth, 1892.

Hoh 1885 Hoh, Theodor. *Die Stellung der Atomenlehre zur Physik des Aethers. Geschichtlich-physikalische Studie.* Bamberg: Gärtner, 1885.

Jungnickel and McCormmach 1986 Jungnickel, Christa, and McCormmach, Russell. *Intellectual Mastery of Nature: Theoretical Physics from Ohm to Einstein.* Vol. 2, *The Now Mighty Theoretical Physics 1870–1925.* Chicago: University of Chicago Press, 1986.

Kayser 1930 Kayser, Rudolf [Anton Reiser, pseud.]. *Albert Einstein: A Biographical Portrait.* New York: Boni, 1930.

Kayser and Runge 1892a Kayser, Heinrich, and Runge, Carl. "Über die Spektren der Elemente. Fünfter Abschnitt. Über die Spektren von Kupfer, Silber und Gold." *Königlich Preußische Akademie der Wissenschaften zu Berlin. Abhandlungen* (1892).

Kayser and Runge 1892b ———. "Über die Spektren der Elemente. Sechster Abschnitt. Über die Spektren von Aluminium, Indium und Thallium." *Königlich Preußische Akademie der Wissenschaften zu Berlin. Abhandlungen* (1892).

Kayser and Runge 1893 ———. "Über die Spektren der Elemente. Siebenter Abschnitt. Die Spektren von Zinn, Blei, Arsen, Antimon, Wismuth." *Königlich Preußische Akademie der Wissenschaften zu Berlin. Abhandlungen* (1893).

Kirchhoff 1894 Kirchhoff, Gustav Robert. *Vorlesungen über mathematische Physik.* Vol. 4, *Theorie der Wärme.* Max Planck, ed. Leipzig: Teubner, 1894.

Kirchhoff 1897 ———. *Vorlesungen über mathematische Physik.* Vol. 1, *Mechanik.* 4th ed. Wilhelm Wien, ed. Leipzig: Teubner, 1897.

Koenigsberger 1901. Koenigsberger, J. "Ueber die Abhängigkeit der Absorption des Lichtes in festen Körpern von der Temperatur." *Annalen der Physik* 4 (1901): 796–810.

Landolt and Bornstein 1894 Landolt, Hans, and Börnstein, Richard. *Physikalisch-chemische Tabellen.* 2d ed. Berlin: Springer, 1894.

Lang 1900 Lang, Robert. "Ueber die magnetische Kraft der Atome." *Annalen der Physik* 2 (1900): 483–494.

Lenard 1900 Lenard, Philipp. "Erzeugung von Kathodenstrahlen durch ultra-violettes Licht." *Annalen der Physik* 2 (1900): 359–375.

Lorentz 1895 Lorentz, Hendrik Antoon. *Versuch einer Theorie der elektrischen und optischen Erscheinungen in bewegten Körpern.* Leiden: Brill, 1895.

Mach 1896 Mach, Ernst. *Die Prinzipien der Wärmelehre. Historisch-kritisch entwickelt.* Leipzig: Barth, 1896.

Mach 1897 ———. *Die Mechanik in ihrer Entwicklung. Historisch-kritisch dargestellt.* 3d ed. Leipzig: Brockhaus, 1897.

Meyer 1877 Meyer, Oskar Emil. *Die kinetische Theorie der Gase. In elementarer Darstellung mit mathematischen Zusätzen.* Breslau: Maruschke & Berendt, 1877.

Meyer 1895 ———. *Die kinetische Theorie der Gase. In elementarer Darstellung mit mathematischen Zusätzen.* 2d ed. Vol. 1. Breslau: Maruschke & Berendt, 1895.

Meyer 1899 ———. *Die kinetische Theorie der Gase. In elementarer Darstellung mit mathematischen Zusätzen.* 2d ed. Vol. 2. Breslau: Maruschke & Berendt, 1899.

Morf 1963 Morf, Hans. *75 Jahre Eidgenössisches Amt für geistiges Eigentum 1888–1963. Jubiläumsschrift.* Bern: [Eidgenössisches Amt für geistiges Eigentum], 1963.

Müller-Pouillet 1888–1890 Müller, Johann, and Pouillet, C. S. *Lehrbuch der Physik und Meteorologie.* 9th rev. ed. Leopold Pfaundler, ed. Vol. 3. Braunschweig: Vieweg, 1888–1890.

Nernst 1898 Nernst, Walther. *Theoretische Chemie vom Standpunkte der Avogadro'schen Regel und der Thermodynamik.* 2d ed. Stuttgart: Enke, 1898.

Ostwald 1891 Ostwald, Wilhelm. *Lehrbuch der allgemeinen Chemie.* Vol. 1, *Stöchiometrie.* 2d rev. ed. Leipzig: Engelmann, 1891.

Ostwald 1893 ———. *Lehrbuch der allgemeinen Chemie.* Vol. 2, *Chemische Energie.* 2d rev. ed. Leipzig: Engelmann, 1893.

Planck 1889 Planck, Max. "Zur Theorie der Thermoelectrizität in metallischen Leitern." *Annalen der Physik und Chemie* 36 (1889): 624–643.

Planck 1897 ———. *Vorlesungen über Thermodynamik.* Leipzig: Veit, 1897.

Planck 1900a ———. "Ueber irreversible Strahlungsvorgänge." *Annalen der Physik* 1 (1900): 69–122.

Planck 1900b ———. "Entropie und Temperatur strahlender Wärme." *Annalen der Physik* 1 (1900): 719–737.

Planck 1900c ———. "Zur Theorie des Gesetzes der Energieverteilung im Normalspectrum." *Deutsche Physikalische Gesellschaft. Verhandlungen* 2 (1900): 237–245.

Planck 1901 ———. "Ueber das Gesetz der Energieverteilung im Normalspectrum." *Annalen der Physik* 4 (1901): 553–563.

Planck 1902 ———. "Zur elektromagnetischen Theorie der Dispersion in isotropen Nichtleitern." *Königlich Preußische Akademie der Wissenschaften zu Berlin. Sitzungsberichte* (1902): 470–494.

Reinganum 1900 Reinganum, Max. "Theoretische Bestimmung des Verhältnisses von Wärme- und Elektricitätsleitung der Metalle aus der Drude'schen Elektronentheorie." *Annalen der Physik* 2 (1900): 398–403.

Riecke 1898 Riecke, Eduard. "Zur Theorie des Galvanismus und der Wärme." *Annalen der Physik und Chemie* 66 (1898): 353–389, 545–581.

Schneider 1965 Schneider, Franz. "Albert Einstein in Schaffhausen." *Schaffhauser Mappe* 33 (1965): 25.

Schopenhauer 1851 Schopenhauer, Arthur. *Parerga und Paralipomena: Kleine philosophische Schriften.* 2 vols. Berlin: Hayn, 1851.

Solovine 1956 Solovine, Maurice, ed. and trans. *Albert Einstein: Lettres à Maurice Solovine.* Paris: Gauthier-Villars, 1956.

Talmey 1932 Talmey, Max. *The Relativity Theory Simplified and the Formative Period of Its Inventor.* New York: Falcon, 1932.

Thomson 1851 Thomson, William. "On a Mechanical Theory of Thermo-Electric Currents" (15 December 1851). *Proceedings of the Royal Society of Edinburgh* 3 (December 1850–April 1857): 91–98.

Voigt 1902 Voigt, Woldemar. "Elektronenhypothese und Theorie des Magnetismus." *Annalen der Physik* 9 (1902): 115–146.

Weber 1881 Weber, Heinrich Friedrich. "Die Beziehungen zwischen dem Wärmeleitungsvermögen und dem elektrischen Leitungsvermögen der Metalle." *Königlich Preußische Akademie der Wissenschaften zu Berlin. Monatsberichte* (for 1880) (1881): 457–478.

Wien, M. 1901 Wien, Max. "Ueber die Erzeugung und Messung von Sinusströmen." *Annalen der Physik* 4 (1901): 425–449.

Wien 1898 Wien, Wilhelm. "Ueber die Fragen, welche die translatorische Bewegung des Lichtäthers betreffen." *Annalen der Physik und Chemie* 65, no. 3, Beilage (1898): i–xvii.

Wien 1908 ———. "Elektromagnetische Lichttheorie." In *Encyklopädie der mathematischen Wissenschaften. Mit Einschluss ihrer Anwendungen.* Vol. 5, part 3. Arnold Sommerfeld, ed. Leipzig: Teubner, 1909–1926.

Winkelmann 1893a Winkelmann, Adolph. "Ueber die specifischen Wärmen verschieden zusammengesetzter Gläser." *Annalen der Physik und Chemie* 49 (1893): 401–420.

Winkelmann 1893b Winkelmann, Adolph, ed. *Handbuch der Physik.* Vol. 3, part 1, *Elektricität und Magnetismus I.* Breslau: Tredwendt, 1893.

Winkelmann 1896 ———. *Handbuch der Physik.* Vol. 2, part 2, *Wärme.* Breslau: Tredwendt, 1896.

Winteler-Einstein 1924 Winteler-Einstein, Maja. "Albert Einstein. Beitrag für sein Lebensbild." Typescript. 15 February 1924.

Wüllner 1896 Wüllner, Adolph. *Lehrbuch der Experimentalphysik.* 5th rev. ed. Vol. 2, *Die Lehre von der Wärme.* Leipzig: Teubner, 1896.

CPSIA information can be obtained
at www.ICGtesting.com
Printed in the USA
BVOW01s2359230117
474268BV00001B/18/P